No-Pattern Knits

Pat Ashforth | Steve Plummer

No-Pattern Knits

SIMPLE MODULAR TECHNIQUES FOR MAKING WONDERFUL GARMENTS AND ACCESSORIES

First edition for the United States, its territories and
dependencies, and Canada published in 2006 by
Barron's Educational Series, Inc.

All inquiries should be addressed to:
Barron's Educational Series, Inc.
250 Wireless Boulevard
Hauppauge, New York 11788
www.barronseduc.com

ISBN-13: 978-0-7641-5892-6
ISBN-10: 0-7641-5892-9

Library of Congress Control No. 2004118229

QUAR.CZK

Conceived, designed, and produced by
Quarto Publishing plc
The Old Brewery
6 Blundell Street
London N7 9BH

Editor Donna Gregory
Designer Elizabeth Healey
Assistant art director Penny Cobb
Picture researcher Claudia Tate
Text editor Eleanor Holme
Proofreader Diana Chambers
Photographer Martin Norris
Illustrators Kuo Kang Chen, Terry Evans, Luise Roberts
Projects Luise Roberts

Art director Moira Clinch
Publisher Paul Carslake

Manufactured by Modern Age Repro House Ltd,
Hong Kong
Printed by SNP Leefung Printing International Ltd, China

9 8 7 6 5 4 3 2 1

Contents

Introduction

No-Pattern Knits will enable you to look at garment shapes in a new way, then make small shapes to create whatever you want without a pattern. There are suggestions for a great deal of experimenting, and also complete projects for those who still require a little more guidance.

Start at the beginning, and after reading the first few pages, you will have learned enough to make a sweater or jacket using the simplest modular techniques. After that, there are many points where you may feel compelled to stop and make something. This book could last a knitting lifetime.

Over time, you can work through all the extra information, but you should also be prepared to abandon the book and "do your own thing" when your own ideas start to take over.

The individual modules require very basic knitting skills and are guaranteed to fit together using your own choice of yarn. The challenge lies in looking at the shapes of garments and other items in a new way to see how they can be broken down into modules.

Creations can be very economical to make, as scraps, odd balls, and small quantities of exotic yarns can all be used to good effect.

This is an inexpensive way of working as you can use any yarns and any needles. If you have already been knitting for some time, you probably won't need to buy anything, but you will find tips for buying and making yarns that you might not have thought of before. If you are new to knitting, you will be able to start with a couple of balls of basic yarn.

The knitting requires very basic techniques, but the methods for creating designs will prove equally exciting for novice and experienced knitters alike.

What is modular knitting?

Modular knitting is a fun way to make unique garments, and fashion and home accessories—without knitting patterns.

It will change the way you look at shapes and how they combine to create an infinite variety of items, all using your own choice of yarns. This approach appeals to new and experienced knitters alike, as there are no difficult stitches to learn. Best of all, this method guarantees that anything you knit will fit, whether you're knitting for a baby, a friend, or your partner. You'll never need another knitting pattern again, but beware—modular knitting can be addictive!

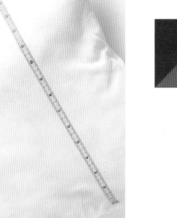

1 Arm yourself with yarn and needles
⇨ **See pages 12–13**

You can use any yarn and any needles. If you are already a knitter, you will probably have plenty of suitable yarns. If you are a beginner, buy a couple of balls of inexpensive plain DK-weight yarn, and the needles suggested on the ball band.

2 Take measurements
⇨ **See pages 64–65**

Arm yourself with a tape measure. Depending on what you want to knit, find an existing item whose size and shape you want to recreate (for example, a favorite sweater or a sofa cushion). Use the existing item to decide how big you want the modular item to be. Measure its length and width, and add or take off the amount needed to make it the size you want.

3 How many squares?
⇨ **See pages 65**

Do you want large square blocks or small square blocks, half-square blocks or a mixture? The choice is yours. Figure out how many of your chosen block size will fit into the width and length of the item you measured in step 2. You'll need a calculator for this step, but this part isn't difficult.

4 Draw the squares
⇨ **See pages 66–67**

Draw a scaled-down version of what you plan to knit and mark in the square blocks that will fill the shape. Draw one full-size square to use as a measure or template.

5 Knit the squares
⇨ **See pages 20–21**

Start with one stitch at the corner and increase at the beginning of every row until the knitting fits the widest part of the template, then decrease at the end of every row until all the stitches have gone.

6 Join the squares
⇨ **See pages 22–27**

Place two squares face to face and overcast (whip stitch) them together using a large sewing needle and the yarn you have been knitting with. Stitch all the squares for each row, then stitch the rows together.

7 Finished knit
A knitted cushion made in a simple garter stitch using coordinating colors.

modular knitting basics

CHAPTER ONE

In this chapter...

Materials and equipment

The most important ingredients for No-Pattern Knits are imagination and a sense of adventure. You need an open mind and a willingness to look at shapes in a new way.

You can't go out and buy these ingredients, but you can buy beautiful, practical yarns and equipment to start you on your way to modular knitting. You may well already have favorite yarns and tools, and these can be added to as you go along. Don't be afraid to experiment with yarns, and you will soon discover great new combinations of colors, shapes, and textures!

Bulky (chunky) wool/acrylic
Aran-weight Shetland wool
Bulky (chunky) wool
Aran-weight wool
Aran-weight cotton/angora
DK-weight wool/acrylic
Sport-weight cotton/acrylic
Fingering-weight wool
DK-weight cotton
Fingering-weight wool

Yarn

Let your imagination take over. There are thousands of yarns to choose from, but you can mix and match them to your heart's content. Use two or three colors for a subtle effect; try a dozen shades of one color; perhaps use twenty or thirty colors from your collection, with a neutral or contrast to tie them all together; choose one beautiful color and create interest and variety by using different textures; experiment with a variegated or self-striping yarn for unique effects. Choose any yarn in any thickness or fiber, bearing in mind two simple rules:

■ Although it is possible to mix the weights of yarn used, the instructions in this book assume that you will be using the same weight throughout a project. For example, use all DK-weight yarn.

■ Your finished garment must be washed according to the most gentle instructions on any of the ball bands.

Yarns for free

Tie short lengths of yarn together to make a unique and unpredictable yarn of your own. Choose each new length in a color close to the previous one to achieve a subtle effect.

Recycle yarn from worn out or outgrown garments. Unravel the garments, wind the yarn into small hanks, wash and allow to dry so that the kinks drop out, then wind into balls for knitting. As you will mostly be creating small pieces of knitting, it won't matter if the balls are much smaller than you would normally work with.

Yarn storage

Store unused balls and scraps of yarn away from dust and dampness in transparent plastic bags or boxes, sorting them by weight, fiber content, and color. An organized collection of odd balls and remnants is a no-pattern knitter's best friend.

Needles

The range of knitting needles available is enormous and you can use almost any type for modular knitting, according to your particular preference. Much of the time you will be working with only a small number of stitches, so very small needles, like those intended for children, are perfect for some knitters. These have the advantage of being small enough to carry a project with you for working on in odd moments.

Circular needles are equally useful. They don't have to be used for knitting "in the round." They are just as good for flat knitting and there is never any fear of losing a needle. These needles are very versatile as you can also use them when you want to work on the same item with a larger number of stitches, such as for bands and edgings.

Any straight needles can be used, but remember that small pieces need to be turned very frequently and long needles have more chance of getting tangled when you turn.

You might find double-pointed needles useful if you are experienced with them, but novices should take care not to lose stitches off the unprotected ends.

Most yarns now carry information on their bands recommending sizes (thickness) of needles, and it is best to be guided by this to start with. However, as you get more adventurous you may decide to disregard it entirely.

Whatever size you choose, you will often need one needle two or three sizes bigger for binding off loosely.

Needle care
- Needles should be kept clean and dry, stored flat with the points protected.
- Plastic and aluminum needles may be washed in warm water if necessary.
- Damaged needles will snag the yarn as you knit—replace them.

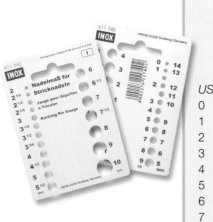

Equivalent needle sizes

Needles are sized in the US from 0 to 50, and in Europe from 2 mm to 15 mm or more. There is not an exact match between the two systems.

US	EUROPE	US	EUROPE
0	2 mm	9	5.5 mm
1	2.25 mm	10	6 mm
2	2.75 mm	10½	6.5 or 7 mm
3	3.25 mm	11	8 mm
4	3.5 mm	13	9 mm
5	3.75 mm	15	10 mm
6	4 mm	17	12.75 mm
7	4.5 mm	19	15 mm
8	5 mm		

Other equipment

If you are already a knitter, you probably own most of the equipment you need. If you are a beginner, there are a few extras you may wish to acquire along the way, though it is probable that you already have basic tools such as scissors, pins (non-rusting), and safety-pins.

Crochet hook

A crochet hook with similar thickness to your needles, may be useful at times, especially for joining shapes together (see page 24).

Sewing-up needles

Look for needles with large eyes and blunt tips to prevent splitting strands of yarn. They are sold as "yarn needles" or "tapestry needles," and are available in a wide range of sizes to suit any type of yarn.

Stitch markers

These can be bought or you can use loops of contrasting yarn to mark points you may need to locate later.

Large-headed pins

Use these to hold knitted pieces together. Large heads prevent the pins from being lost between the stitches.

Tape measure and ruler

Buy a new tape measure from time to time, as old ones stretch with use and become inaccurate. A ruler is useful for accurately measuring dimensions.

Small sharp scissors

Always use scissors for cutting yarn, never break it between your fingers.

Stitch holders

These are like huge safety pins. Use them for temporarily holding stitches, such as the neckband stitches on a sweater.

Equivalent weights and measures

US	UK & EUROPE
¾ ounce	20 grams
1 ounce	28 grams
1¾ ounces	50 grams
2 ounces	60 grams
3½ ounces	100 grams
1 inch	2.5 centimeters
4 inches	10 centimeters
39½ inches	1 meter
1 yard	91.5 centimeters

Basic techniques

The basic techniques that you will need in order to start knitting take only minutes to learn, and they will serve you for a **lifetime of knitting. Use the techniques shown here, or ask someone to show you how to get started.**

Slip knot

Every piece of knitting begins with a slip knot.

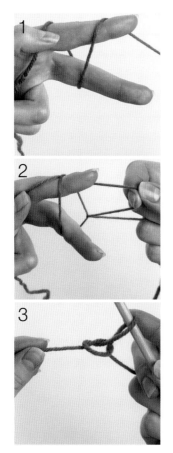

1 Unwind about 12 inches (30 cm) of yarn from the ball and place the tail to your left and the ball to your right. Wind the ball end clockwise around two fingers of your left hand.

2 Pull a loop from the ball end through the loop on your fingers, from behind.

3 Slip the tip of one needle through the new loop from front to back. Tighten the knot by pulling on the tail and the ball end at the same time. This is the first stitch for any cast-on method.

Holding yarn and needles

There are many ways to hold your yarn and needles, so it's up to you to use whichever method you prefer. Here are just two ways: the English method is the one used for the photographs in this book, but you may find holding the yarn in your left hand (the Continental method) more comfortable.

The English (right-hand) method

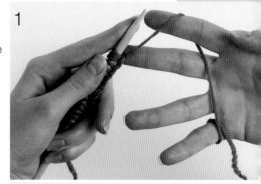

1 Hold the needle with the stitches in your left hand. Your forefinger should be close to the needle tip, with the other three fingers supporting the needle. Put the little finger of your right hand behind the yarn, twist your hand to loop the yarn around your little finger, then lift the yarn with your forefinger, as shown.

2 Pick up the empty needle with your right hand and hold it with your forefinger close to the tip and the other three fingers supporting the needle from below. To wrap the yarn for a stitch, move your right forefinger forward without completely letting go of the needle.

The Continental (left-hand) method

1 Hold the needle with the stitches in your right hand, with your forefinger close to the needle tip, and your other fingers supporting the needle. Put your left little finger behind the yarn, turn your hand to loop the yarn around your little finger, then lift the yarn with your forefinger, as shown.

2 Transfer this needle to your left hand, and pick up the empty needle in your right hand. Both needles are held with the forefinger near the tip and the other three fingers underneath. Rather than wrap the yarn for a stitch, you catch it with the right needle tip, turning your hands slightly with the palms toward you.

Cable cast-on

1 Make a slip knot (see page 15). Hold the needle with the knot in your left hand and the other needle in your right. Insert the tip of the right needle into the front of the loop from left to right. Wind the ball end of yarn counterclockwise around the tip of this needle, as indicated by the arrow.

2 Pull the new loop toward you, through the old loop.

3 Insert the tip of the left-hand needle into the new loop from right to left, and let the new loop slip off the right needle onto the left needle. Now you have two stitches on the left needle.

4 Insert the tip of the right needle under the left needle, between the stitch you just made and the one before. Wind the yarn counterclockwise around the right needle.

5 Pull the new loop through and slip it onto the left needle. Now you will have three stitches on the left needle.

6 Repeat steps 4 and 5 until you have the correct number of stitches.

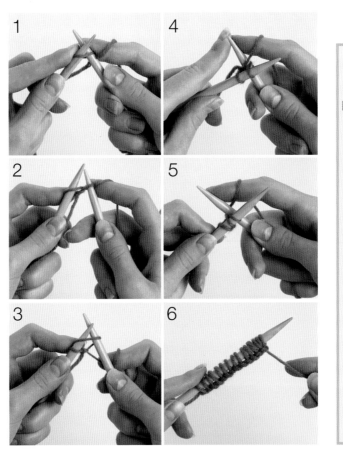

Tip

◼ If you require a firmer edge, such as when beginning a garment with garter stitch, work the two-needle cable cast-on as given, then work the first row through the back loops of the stitches instead of the front. This tightens the stitches by twisting them.

Knit a row

If you knit every stitch of every row, or purl every stitch of every row, the result is garter stitch. This is the easiest way to knit your shapes.

1 Slip the right needle tip from left to right into the first stitch on the left needle, below the tip of the left needle and in front of the yarn held in your right hand. Take care not to split the stitch with the point of the needle.

2 For the English method, use your right forefinger to carry the yarn counterclockwise around the right needle and between the two needles from left to right. (For the Continental method, catch the yarn from the right with the right needle tip.)

3 Use the right needle tip to pull the loop of yarn toward you, through the first stitch on the left needle.

4 Slip the first stitch off the left needle. One knit stitch is on the right needle.

5 Repeat steps 1, 2, 3, and 4. Every few stitches, push the stitches on the right needle down from the tip to prevent them bunching together in your right hand, and push the stitches on the left needle up toward the tip. When all the stitches from the left needle have been knitted onto the right needle, you have made one row of knit stitches. Move the needle with the stitches to your left hand to begin the next row.

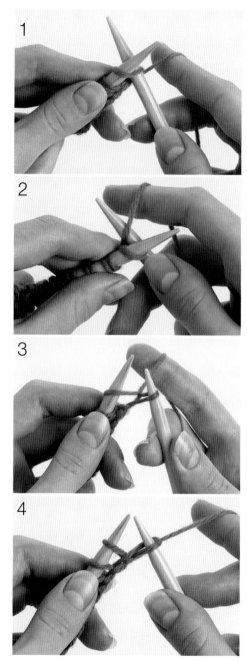

Buttonholes

Buttonholes are often worked by binding off a group of stitches on one row (see page 19), then casting the same number on again on the next row (see page 16). When casting on the new stitches, before you slip the last one onto the left needle, bring the yarn between the needles, to the side of the work facing you, then transfer the last cast-on stitch to the left needle. This will tighten the stitch and make a neater buttonhole.

Purl a row

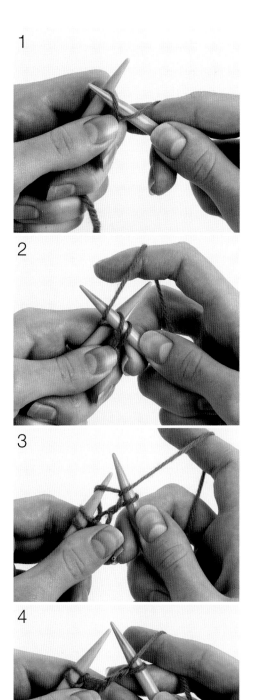

1 Hold the needle with the stitches in your left hand, and the empty needle in your right hand, as before. Hold the yarn in front of the right needle and insert the right needle tip into the first stitch on the left needle, from right to left, in front of the left needle.

2 Use your right forefinger to wrap the yarn counterclockwise around the right needle tip as shown. (For the Continental method, use your left forefinger to wrap the yarn counterclockwise.)

3 With the right needle tip, pull the loop of yarn away from you, through the first stitch.

4 Slip the first stitch off the left needle. One purl stitch is on the right needle.

5 Repeat steps 1 to 4 until all the stitches from the left needle have been worked onto the right needle. You have made one row of purl stitches. Notice how the purl row forms a row of loops on the side of the work facing you. Move the needle with the stitches to your left hand to begin the next row.

Stitch increases

There are several ways of creating extra stitches but this increase will produce the smoothest edge to the basic square.

1 Knit to the position of the increase, knit into the next stitch on the left-hand needle as usual but without slipping it off the needle.

2 Then insert the right needle into the same stitch again but this time into the back of the stitch and complete to stitch as if to knit. Slip the stitch off the left-hand needle.

Knit two together (abbr. K2tog)

By knitting two stitches together, you create a right-slanting decrease.

1 Insert the right needle through the fronts of two stitches on the left needle from left to right. Wrap the yarn in the usual way for a knit stitch.

2 Draw the new loop through and drop both stitches together from the left needle.

Purl two together (abbr. P2tog)

Worked on a wrong side row, this decrease also creates a right-slanting decrease on the right side of the work.

1 Insert the tip of the right needle from right to left through two stitches on the left needle.

2 Wrap the yarn in the usual way for a purl stitch.

3 Draw the new loop through, away from you, and allow both stitches to drop from the left needle.

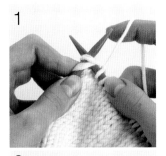

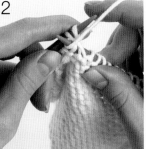

Binding off

Binding off links stitches together at the end of a piece of knitting. You might need to bind off all the stitches, or just a certain number (for example, for an armhole shaping or a buttonhole). A bound-off edge should not be too loose or too tight. It should stretch by about the same amount as the rest of the piece. If you need a looser, more elastic edge, for example, on a neckband, change to a needle one or two sizes larger than the previous rows.

1 Knit the first two stitches in the usual way onto the right needle. Insert the tip of the left needle from left to right into the front of the first stitch you knitted.

2 Lift the first stitch over the second stitch and off the right needle. One stitch remains on the right needle. You have bound off one stitch. Knit the next stitch. There are now two stitches

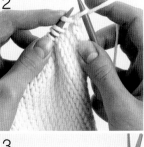
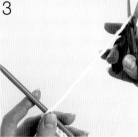
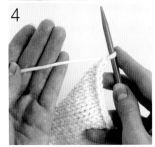

on the right needle. Repeat step 2 as required.

3 When you bind off all the stitches, you will be left with one stitch on the right needle. Cut the yarn, leaving a tail of at least 6 inches (15 cm).

4 Wrap the tail around the right needle, lift the last stitch over it and pull the tail through to make a neat finish.

How to knit squares

By knitting diagonally, it is very easy to make perfect squares, of the size you want in any yarn. The squares are guaranteed to fit together even when they are made by two or more knitters working on different needles and at a different gauge (tension). You can forget about working to a particular gauge and use a variety of yarns. The squares will still be the correct size. With yarn, needles, and a paper template, you can't go wrong.

The perfect square lies flat so you can measure it easily, has no loopy edges that make it difficult to join, and has nothing to spoil its appearance.

template

Checklist for the perfect square

First, decide on the size you want the square and make a paper template to these dimensions.

1 Knit in garter stitch and have your paper template nearby.
2 On every row knit to the end of the row and knit the last stitch twice to increase the stitches.
3 A triangle starts to appear.
4 Check the triangle against the template.
5 Don't cheat! Don't stretch! When the ends of the triangle match your template, you can start decreasing the stitches.
6 On every row, knit to the last two stitches, then knit the last two together.
7 When you have only two stitches left, knit them together and bind off.
8 You have the perfect square.

Good squares

These squares are all the same dimensions and will look good when the edges are joined together.

Right-for-its-job square
Good squares are tidy and feel right for their purpose. A sweater will need to be soft; a bag may need to be sturdier.

Good-use-of-template square
Use the template carefully and all the squares will match, regardless of the yarn you choose.

Mixing yarns
You can change yarn from one square to the next. The squares will be exactly the same size, provided they have been knitted diagonally.

Needle sizes

■ If your square is too loose, use smaller needles. If the square is too stiff, choose larger needles.

Poor squares

Loopy squares
Squares with loops along the edge are very difficult to join together. The loops form holes and distract from the precise lines of the squares.

Distorted squares Some increases and decreases distort the edges of the squares, which will spoil their appearance. Edges should be as straight as possible.

Joining shapes

In most conventional knitting patterns, the pieces have extra stitches at the edges for making seams. The shapes in this book do not. They lie edge-to-edge, which is why you can be sure you will finish with the size you want. The edges must not be allowed to overlap at all. There will be no bulky seams and the back of the work will look almost as good as the front.

Coaxing squares into shape

Garter stitch is usually very good-natured. The edges never curl and it will need little blocking to form perfect squares. In many cases a good tug is enough to form a perfect shape. The main exception to this is yarns that have a flat cross-section, such as chenille or ribbon. These may require more coaxing.

Blocking your shapes using an iron in the usual way is not recommended as it will flatten the bumps in the garter stitch and destroy the texture you have created. If you have to block the shapes, try the gentlest methods first.

Spraying and shaping

If you plan to block many shapes, consider making a padded board covered with a check fabric where the shapes can be lined up with the pattern on the fabric. The padding can be old blankets, polyester batting, foam or anything else suitable for sticking pins into.

Small pieces can be shaped very successfully on a piece of polystyrene packaging. Use your knitting template to mark the same size on the polystyrene. Spray the shape with water (or immerse in water and remove the excess in a towel, if no spray is available). Place the shape on the polystyrene template and insert a pin at each corner. Place the pins at an angle leaning out from the shape. Add extra pins at the center of each side, and more pins between these, if necessary. Allow to dry.

Steaming and shaping

Very firm shapes may need stronger treatment. Pin the shape in the way just described above and use a steam iron to give blasts of steam to the shape, without actually touching it with the iron. If you have a steam iron with a built-in spray, you can combine the spraying and steaming processes.

Blocking with heat

If all other methods fail to produce perfect squares, use your iron over a clean cloth or absorbent paper towels to press the edges of the square lightly. Be aware that heat will damage some yarns, so pay special attention to any information on the ball bands. Do not use heat if you have used polystyrene, or any other plastic, for your blocking template.

Joining by stitching

Garter stitch squares, and other shapes, are very easy to stitch together because the edges are always flat. Even if you normally dislike sewing up a completed garment, do not be afraid to join many small pieces together. The two main methods of stitching are from the back and from the front. Whip stitch is extremely easy, especially for novice sewers. Mattress stitch has the advantage of your being able to see the outcome of every stitch you make.

Whip stitch

This method of sewing from the back is also known as overcasting.

1 Place two squares together with their right sides facing and their corners matching exactly. If you have long lengths of yarn at the corners of your shapes, use them for stitching. Otherwise, use a length of yarn to match one of the squares and attach it firmly to the first corner.

2 Whip stitch over the edge of both squares, working far enough into the squares to make sure they are secure, but not far enough to stop them from lying flat, side by side, when you open them up.

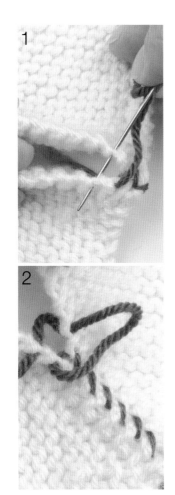

Mattress stitch

Place the two shapes side by side. If they are large pieces, or have special points that must be linked, you may want to use safety-pins to hold them loosely together.

1 Use any connected yarns, or securely attach a new length of yarn. Start at the bottom edge and pass the needle through the top of the first stitch on one square, then through the bottom of the matching stitch on the other square.

2 Work a few stitches in this way, then pull the yarn gently until the stitches close together, giving an almost-invisible join. Continue until the whole seam is closed, then bind off.

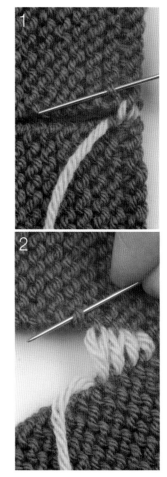

Tips for joining

■ The order in which you join the squares will vary from one project to another. Some ways might be easier than others, but the end result will be the same. It is particularly important to match corners, whether they point inward or outward. Sometimes the corners seem to need more stretching than other parts. Flatten or smooth them out as you stitch rather than allowing them to form bulges or hollows.

■ When all of the shapes are squares, it is generally easier to join them into rows first, and then to join the rows together.

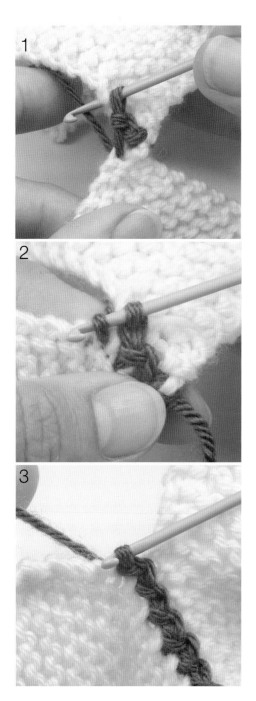

1

2

3

Joining by crochet

Crocheting shapes together is a dual-purpose method. It joins the shapes and gives a decorative finish. It is not a good idea to put the pieces back-to-back and crochet through both pieces. This creates a seam that falls to one side or the other, and can distort your item or make it look unbalanced.

1 Place the squares side by side and work with the joining yarn at the back and the hook at the front. Make a slip knot and pull it through to the front with the hook.

2 Insert the hook into the corresponding stitch on the other square, pull a loop of yarn through the block, and then loop on the hook.

3 Continue in this way, alternating between the squares, pulling through a loop each time. When you get to the end, break off the yarn, pull the end through the last loop, and fasten it securely by pulling the end through a few of the stitches at the back.

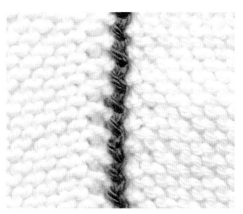

Two sample squares joined together using crochet. A contrast yarn is used for clarity.

Diagonal	Edge	Diagonal	Edge
10	7	25	18
11	8	26	18
12	8	27	19
13	9	28	20
14	10	29	21
15	11	30	21
16	11	31	22
17	12	32	23
18	13	33	23
19	13	34	24
20	14	35	25
21	15	36	25
22	16	37	26
23	16	38	27
24	17	39	28

This chart tells you the number of stitches you need for the side of the square, when you know the number of stitches in the diagonal.

Joining shapes as you work

There are many instances where a new shape can be knitted directly onto an existing shape and you will need to pick up stitches from the first shape. There are three ways to do this: picking up stitches from the edge of diagonally knitted square; picking up stitches along the edge of a straight piece of knitting, or picking up one stitch at a time from an existing shape.

Picking up stitches from the edge of a diagonally knitted square

Work out the number of stitches you need to pick up from the edge of the square by using the chart on page 26. Pick up these stitches, taking care to get the first and last stitches at the corners, as follows:

1 With the right side of the shape facing, insert only one needle into the firm part of the knot at the end of the ridge. Pull through a loop of yarn and keep it on the right-hand needle to create the first stitch. Repeat in the second ridge.

2 In the same way, pick up a stitch in the end of the furrow before the next ridge, pulling the yarn through the firmest part so that you don't create a hole. If you have difficulty picking up the stitches with your knitting needle, pull each loop of yarn through using a crochet hook and slip the loops onto your knitting needle as you go.

3 Pick up one stitch from each of the third and fourth ridges. As in step 2, pick up a stitch in the end of the furrow before the next ridge, pulling the yarn through the firmest part. Pick up one stitch. You should now have seven stitches. Repeat for each set of five ridges.

The ridges formed from the pickup stitches will create a horizontal ridged square.

Picking up stitches from a straight edge

The width of one stitch, in garter stitch, is equal to the height of one garter ridge. (A ridge is made up of two rows.) If your knitting has a completely straight edge, pick up one stitch from the end of each of the ridges.

1 Pick up one stitch from each of the cast-off stitches.

2 You should now have picked up all the stitches.

3 This shows the beginning of the new square, from the picked-up stitches.

The ridges on the new square are in the same direction as the first.

1

2

3

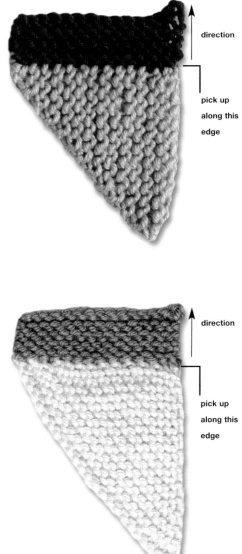

direction

pick up
along this
edge

direction

pick up
along this
edge

Picking up one stitch at a time from an existing shape

There are three different circumstances when you might want to use this technique.

1 You need an extra stitch. Instead of increasing at the end of the row in the usual way, pick up the extra stitch from the corresponding ridge of the existing shape.

2 You need to keep the same number of stitches as before. Pick up one stitch from the existing piece. (You now have one more stitch than you need.) At the start of the next row, knit two together. Using this method, the join on the wrong side looks as good as that on the right side.

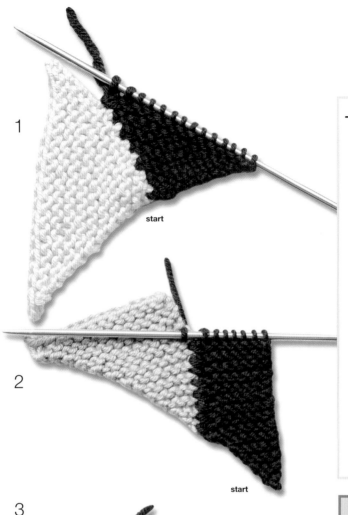

1

start

2

start

3

start

3 You need to decrease by one. Knit together the last two stitches of the row, where it is about to join the existing piece. Pick up one from the existing piece. (You now have the same number of stitches as before.) At the start of the next row, slip the first stitch, knit the second stitch, and pass the slipped stitch over. In some yarns this join can be rather bulky and may be better left unjoined, then stitched later.

Tip

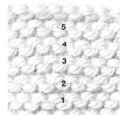

As a general rule, every five ridges of garter stitch has to produce seven stitches. Five of these are from the ends of the ridges and the others from between ridges 1 and 2, and ridges 4 and 5.

GETTING THE CORRECT NUMBER OF STITCHES

Divide the number of stitches you had at the widest part (the diagonal) of your square by 1.4. Round the answer to the nearest whole number. This is the number of stitches needed along the side of the square.

Square variations

Squares don't have to be plain and uninteresting. Spectacular designs can be made by using two, or more, colors in each square and then arranging the squares in different ways. You will be **surprised by the number of patterns you can create with a batch of similar squares. Try various arrangements with your squares before you reach a final decision about your design.**

Make the first half of the square, increasing one stitch at the end of every row. Break off the yarn, leaving a long end for seaming. Using the second color, knit one row even. Complete the square by decreasing at the end of every row.

Sawtooth—all squares in the same orientation.

Windmills—repeated block of four squares.

Large pinwheel—rotated block of four squares.

Eight-pointed star— rotated block of four squares.

Arrowheads—rotated block of four squares.

Light and shadow— block of four in two orientations.

Stripes—alternate up and down squares.

Butterflies—rotated block of four squares.

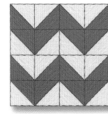

Zigzags—repeated block of four squares.

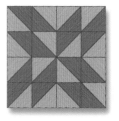

Parallelograms—rotated block of four squares.

Square in square—rotated block of four squares.

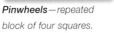

Pinwheels—repeated block of four squares.

Table and chairs— rotated block of four squares.

Using the first color, begin the square as before. Continue until you have half the number of stitches needed at the widest point. Change to the second color and complete the first half of the square. Using the first color, work one row even, then decrease on every row and complete as for a plain square.

Hidden windmill—rotated block of four squares.

Make the first half of the square as above. Change to the first color. Knit one row even, then decrease on every row until you have the same number of stitches as when you changed color on the first half. Complete the square with the second color.

Candy stripes—all squares in the same orientation.

Shadow Xs—repeated block of four squares.

X—block of eight squares and rotation.

Honeycomb—repeated block of four squares.

Catherine wheel—rotated block of four squares.

Split chevrons—repeated block of two squares.

Tip

■ Always change color on the same side of the work.

CHAPTER TWO

making other shapes

In this chapter...

How to knit triangles

A square can be cut in half diagonally to form two identical triangles. The angles of this triangle will always be the same size regardless of the length of the sides.

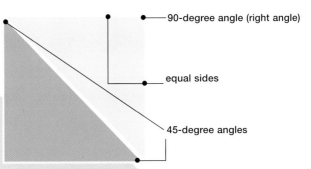

90-degree angle (right angle)

equal sides

45-degree angles

Template

Three methods of knitting a triangle

The first half of the basic square

- Make a slip knot and knit into it twice.
- **Every row**: knit to the last stitch; knit into the last stitch twice.
- Continue until the triangle is the size you want then bind off loosely, using a larger needle. (The edge must not pull tight and distort the triangle.)

Reverse method

If you know how wide the triangle has to be, work the triangles in reverse, starting from the widest part.

- Cast on, or pick up, the required number of stitches.
- **Every row**: knit to the last two stitches; knit two together.
- Continue until two stitches remain. Knit two together.
- Bind off.

Ridges at right angles to half basic square

- Make a slip knot and knit into it twice.
- **Next row**: knit.
- **Next row**: knit to the last stitch; knit into the last stitch twice.
- Repeat these two rows until you reach the half-way point of the triangle.
- **Next row**: knit.
- **Next row**: knit to the last two stitches; knit two together.
- Repeat these two rows until two stitches remain. Knit two together. Bind off.

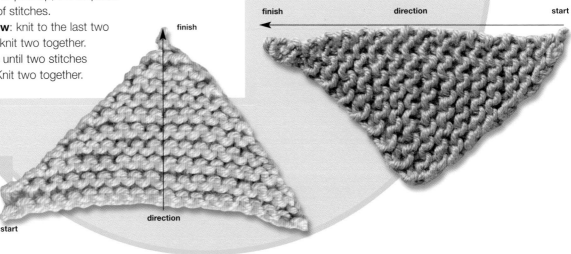

finish   direction   start

finish

direction

start

Increase at one side and keep the other side straight

- Make a slip knot and knit into it twice.
- **Next row**: knit.
- **Next row**: knit to the last stitch; knit into the last stitch twice.
- Repeat these two rows until the triangle is the size you want. Bind off loosely.

Reverse method

If you know how wide the triangle has to be, work the triangles in reverse, starting from the widest part.

- Cast on the required number of stitches.
- **Next row**: knit.
- **Next row**: knit to the last two stitches; knit two together.
- Repeat these two rows until two stitches remain. Knit two together. Bind off.

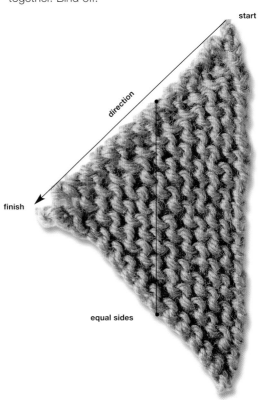

start

direction

finish

equal sides

Combining triangles

Triangles can be combined to form squares. When knitted in different directions, the textures and shadows created by garter stitch ridges create an interesting texture.

Looking in—four rotated squares.

Pinwheels—four rotated squares.

Arrows—four squares in the same orientation.

Corners—four squares rotated.

Criss-cross—four squares in the same orientation.

Looking out—four squares rotated.

Simple shapes with four sides

Many four-sided shapes can be made very easily, using the same simple methods as for making squares. These shapes can be fitted together without any further calculations or complicated shaping. Learn to make these basic shapes and you will be able to combine them in arrangements of your own.

Patterns made by fitting small shapes together are known as tessellations. Once you know how to create the shapes, have fun creating different patterns.

In order to use four-sided shapes, you may need some information about each of them and to know which can be made using the methods learned so far.

Four-sided shapes

A four-sided shape is also called a quadrilateral. The four-sided shapes dealt with in this book are detailed below.

*A **square** has four equal sides and four 90-degree angles (right angles). It has two pairs of parallel sides. See page 20.*

*A **rectangle** has four right angles and two pairs of parallel sides. See page 36.*

*A **lozenge** has four equal sides and two pairs of parallel sides with angles of 45 and 135 degrees. See page 41.*

*A **diamond** is simply a square or rhombus turned to stand on its point.*

*A **parallelogram** has two pairs of parallel sides, with angles of 45 and 135 degrees. It is like a rectangle that has been pushed over. See page 40.*

*A **trapezoid** has one pair of parallel sides. The other two sides can slope inward, outward, or straight up, at angles of 45, 90, or 135 degrees. See page 38.*

Which shapes can you make?

For ease of fit, and to make use of the methods learned so far, use only shapes that have 45- and 90-degree angles.

Squares—any size.

Rectangles—any size.

Rhombuses—any size but only with 45-degree angles.

Parallelograms—any size but only with 45-degree angles.

Trapezoids—any size but only with 45- and 90-degree angles.

Stick to these shapes and it is just as easy to make a random pattern as it is to make a repeating pattern.

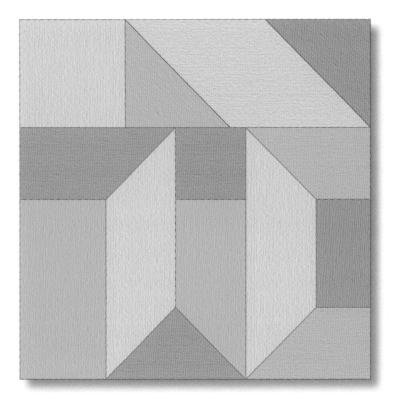

It is very easy to combine all these different shapes. All that matters is that you should make each shape slope in the right direction to fit with the others. The diagrams show how to determine the techniques needed.

Designing other shapes

You already know all the techniques needed to start creating other shapes. There are only three possibilities at each side of the shape: straight, increase, decrease.

The diagrams show all the combinations.

Left: *increase.*
Right: *decrease.*   **Left:** *decrease.*
Right: *decrease.*   **Left:** *decrease.*
Right: *increase.*

Left: *increase.*
Right: *increase.*

Left: *increase.*
Right: *straight.*   **Left:** *straight.*
Right: *increase.*

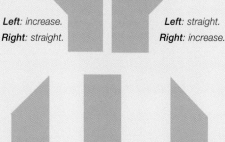

Left: *decrease.*
Right: *straight.*   **Left:** *straight.*
Right: *straight.*   **Left:** *straight.*
Right: *decrease.*

How to knit rectangles

A rectangle is a simple block shape with four square corners and two pairs of parallel sides. A square is a special kind **of rectangle, so most of the rules for knitting a rectangle are the same as those for knitting a square.**

Knitting a rectangle

- Increase at the end of every row, as for the beginning of a square, until the short sides of the triangle are the size you want for the width of your rectangle, finishing at the right-hand side.
- **Next row**: knit to the last stitch; knit into the last stitch twice.
- **Next row**: knit to the last two stitches; knit two together.
- (The left-hand edge continues to slope as before; the right-hand

edge starts to slope in the same direction, creating the parallel sides.)
- Repeat these two rows until the longest edge of the shape is the height of the rectangle you want, finishing at the right-hand side.
- **Next row**: knit to the last two stitches; knit two together.
- Repeat this row until there are two stitches remaining. Knit two together and bind off.

Adding interest
To add textural interest, you may want the garter stitch ridges running in the opposite direction. If you are working with plain rectangles, you can simply turn them over to get the texture you want.

For multicolored rectangles, reverse all shaping.

start

start

start

start

start

finish

finish

finish

finish

finish

▲▶ *Identical rectangles facing opposite ways.*

◀▲ *Two-color rectangles with shaping reversed.*

Fitting rectangles together

Rectangles can be any width and any length. Those that are twice as high as they are wide fit together very well in different directions.

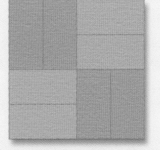

Use rectangles in groups of two to create squares.

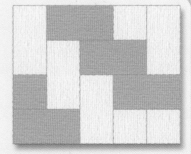

Stagger rectangles to create a step pattern.

Two- and three-color rectangles

Use two colors in each rectangle to make more patterns.

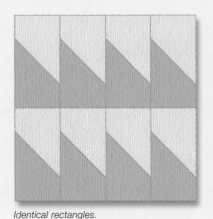

Identical rectangles.

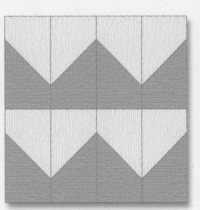

Rectangles made in different directions.

The same rectangles with some turned around.

Add stripes to create even more possibilities.

Rectangles with colored corner and stripe.

Similar rectangles in off-set pattern.

Striped rectangles facing the same way.

37

How to knit trapezoids

A trapezoid has one pair of parallel sides. The other two sides can go in any direction. Using the rules of this book, there is a limit to the number of variations that can be made, though each can be turned around or over. They can be made to any length and width you want. There are two main types:

1 Trapezoids with right angles
2 Trapezoids without right angles

Each type can be knitted in any of three directions, as detailed here.

start

finish

start

finish

Methods for knitting trapezoids with right angles

Starting at the 45-degree point (right, top)
■ Make a slip knot and knit into it twice.
■ **Next row**: knit.
■ **Next row**: knit to the last stitch; knit into the last stitch twice.
■ Repeat these two rows until you have the width you want for the trapezoid.
■ Knit straight until you have the size you want.
■ Bind off loosely.

Reverse method
■ If you know how wide the trapezoid is to be, it can be made starting from the widest part.
■ Cast on the required number of stitches.

■ Knit straight until you reach the point where the slope should begin.
■ **Next row**: knit to the last two stitches; knit two together. Repeat these two rows until two stitches remain. Knit two together.
■ Bind off.

Starting at the 90-degree point (right, center)
■ Increase at the end of every row, as for the beginning of a square, until the short side of the triangle is the size you want for the width of your trapezoid.
■ At one edge, continue increasing in the same way.
■ At the other edge, knit two together at the end of the row. (One edge continues to slope as before; the other edge starts to form a line parallel to it.)

■ Repeat these two rows until the longest edge of the shape is the height of the trapezoid you want.
■ Bind off loosely.

Reverse method
■ Cast on the number of stitches required for the sloping edge and reverse all shaping.

Starting at one of the parallel sides (right, below)
■ Cast on the number of stitches needed for the straight edge.
■ Knit straight at one side and increase or decrease, depending on whether the shape is to get wider or narrower, on alternate rows at the other edge.

finish   start

Methods for knitting trapezoids without right angles

finish

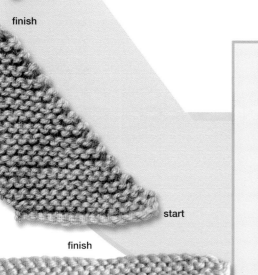

start

Starting at the 45-degree point (left, top)
- Work as for a right angle trapezoid but do not bind off.
- Continue knitting with no shaping at the straight edge and decreasing on alternate rows on the other edge.

Starting at a sloping side (left, center)
- Cast on the number of stitches needed. Increase at one side and decrease at the other until the short side is the correct length.
- Continue to decrease at one side, knit straight at the other until two stitches remain. Knit two together and bind off.

Starting at one of the parallel sides (left, below)
- Cast on the number of stitches needed. Increase or decrease at the end of every row, depending on whether the shape is to get wider or narrower.

finish

start

Mixing shapes

This arrangement is particularly useful because the addition of a small square will create a larger square. These can then be put together to give interesting effects.

How to knit parallelograms and lozenges

A parallelogram has two pairs of parallel sides. Using the methods learned so far, parallelograms can be any length or width but will all slope at the same angle—45 degrees. A lozenge is simply a parallelogram with all four sides of equal length. For our purposes, we will only use lozenges and parallelograms with 45-degree angles. Both shapes are very useful for tessellating.

Knitting a parallelogram

Starting at any of the sides

■ Cast on the number of stitches needed for the straight edge.
■ **Next row**: knit to the last stitch; knit into the stitch twice.
■ **Next row**: knit to the last two stitches; knit two together.
■ Repeat these two rows until the parallelogram is the height you want.
■ Bind off loosely.

Starting at the point

■ Knit straight at one edge; increase at the end of alternate rows at the other edge.
■ When the parallelogram is the width you want, knit straight until the longer edge is the length you want.
■ Continue knitting straight at the shorter edge and decreasing at the other edge.
■ Continue until two stitches remain. Knit two together. Bind off.

finish

start

start

finish

Mixing shapes

Some interesting arrangements can be made using identical lozenges . . . or add squares or triangles in the spaces to make larger motifs.

Rose made entirely from lozenges.

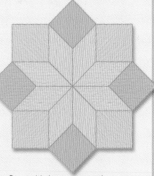

Star with lozenges and squares.

The same design with four of the squares changed to triangles.

Knitting a lozenge

Starting at any of the sides

■ Work as for a parallelogram. To find the height: divide the number of cast on stitches by 1.4 (see table on page 44). The answer tells you the number of garter ridges to knit. Remember that one ridge is two rows of garter stitch.

finish

start

Starting at the point

■ Work as for a parallelogram. When the rhombus is the width you want, count the number of stitches on the needle. Divide this number by 1.4. Knit even for this number of ridges, then decrease at the opposite edge from where you increased, knitting straight at the other edge.

start

finish

Using lozenge strips

■ Narrow strips are useful because you can keep adding more if you change your mind about the size of the garment you are making, and you can use up scraps of yarn.

■ These strips can also be used as a bias binding for edging a garment. They are less bulky than straight strips and can add interest.

■ Take care not to stretch strips. Narrow pieces are much more likely than wider pieces to stretch during construction.

Tessellating parallelograms

Parallelograms and lozenges can easily become plain or colorful strips, with a variety of uses.

A continuous strip of small parallelograms. Use two or more colors for a repeating pattern.

Reverse the shaftings on alternate strips.

Start and end with a triangle to make a long rectangle.

Pick up stitches along the edge of the strip to knit in another direction, or add a border.

How to knit hexagons

It is not possible to make a regular hexagon using the rules learned so far, but you can make an elongated hexagon. The shape is like the two halves of a **square with a straight piece in between. It can be any length and any width. The height of each of the points is half the width of the hexagon.**

Methods for knitting hexagons

Starting at a point

- ■ Start with a slip knot and increase at the end of every row until the hexagon is the width you want.
- ■ Knit straight until the hexagon is the height you want, remembering that the second point will add extra height.
- ■ Decrease at the end of every row until two stitches remain. Knit two together and bind off.

A hexagon is essentially a square or rectangle with a triangle at each end.

finish

start

Starting at an edge parallel to the diagonal between the points

- ■ Cast on the required number of stitches. Increase at the end of every row until the hexagon is the width you want.
- ■ Decrease at the end of every row until you have one more stitch than you had at the start. Bind off, knitting the last two stitches together as you go.

finish

start

Note

- ■ You could knit a hexagon starting at an edge at right angles to a point, but this method is complicated as it varies, depending on the proportions of the hexagon.

finish

start

An elongated hexagon can make an interesting center for a square

■ To add textural interest, and to make the square symmetrical, it is best to start at a point.

■ The total height (from point to point) of the hexagon is the same as the length of the diagonal of the square it is to fit in.

■ The width of the square will be this measurement divided by 1.4. Calculate the number of stitches that would be needed for the diagonal of the square. Make the hexagon by starting at the point. Increase until you have the width you want. Count the stitches on the needle. Subtract this number from the number calculated for the diagonal of the square. Knit straight for this number of garter ridges. Decrease to make the other point.

■ To complete the square: pick up one stitch from each of the straight garter stitch rows and decrease at the end of every row. Repeat on the other side of the hexagon.

Using hexagons as a basis for other shapes

Hexagons can be used as starting shapes. There are many ways to include them in a design.

Vary the width of the hexagons and fit the squares together.

An arrangement of identical hexagons in a range of colors can be very dramatic, and good for using up scraps of yarn.

Try mixing hexagons of different heights, and perhaps some squares.

Turning hexagons at right angles to each other will form a square frame that can be filled in with more hexagons or other shapes.

How to knit octagons

The simple methods used to create shapes so far work because they have been based on using multiples of 1.4. The same methods can be used to make an octagon, combining it with the measurements of a straight square. Octagons are wonderful for adding a little flair to a pattern.

Method for knitting octagons

This shape is a little more difficult to make because all eight sides have to be the same length. The 1.4 rule is very important. Try making this small octagon before you venture on to making other octagons.

Make a practice octagon
- Cast on 10 stitches.
- Knit to the last stitch; knit into the last stitch twice.
- Repeat this row until you have knitted 7 ridges (because 10 divided by 1.4 is 7).
- You will now have 24 stitches.
- Knit straight for 10 ridges (this matches the number of cast on stitches).
- **Next row:** knit to the last two stitches; knit two together.
- Repeat this row until you have 11 stitches (one more than the number of cast on stitches).
- Bind off, knitting the last two stitches together as you go.

Making your own octagon
- To make an octagon to the size you require, the only calculation you need to do is to divide the number of cast on stitches by **1.4**. On the diagram this is called **a/1.4**. The number of cast on stitches is called **a**. Substitute the numbers from your own calculation, or use the chart.

- Cast on your chosen number of stitches (**a** from the diagram).
- Knit **a/1.4** ridges, knitting twice into the last stitch of every row.
- Knit straight for **a** rows.
- Continue, knitting two together at the end of every row until you have one more stitch than you cast on. Bind off, knitting the last two stitches together.

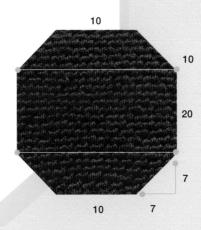

| 10 |
| 10 |
| 20 |
| 7 |
| 10 | 7 |

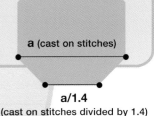

a (cast on stitches)	**a/1.4** (cast on stitches divided by 1.4)
10	7
11	8
12	8
13	9
14	10
15	11
16	11
17	12
18	13
19	13
20	14
21	15
22	16
23	16
24	17
25	18
26	18
27	19
28	20
29	21

a (cast on stitches)

a/1.4
(cast on stitches divided by 1.4)

Note
- 2 rows of garter stitch make 1 ridge.
- 1 ridge is the same width as one stitch.

Fitting octagons

Octagons will not fit on their own, but they can be joined to two other shapes.

Edge-to-edge

When you join the octagons edge-to-edge, you need squares to fill the spaces.

The squares are **a** stitches across their straight edges or **1.4** times **a** across their diagonals.

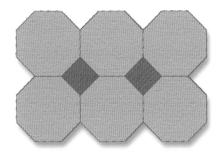

Point-to-point

Join octagons point-to-point and the holes that are left are four-pointed stars.

The angles at the points of the star are 45 degrees, but it is extremely difficult to make the star in one piece (if using only the methods learned so far). However, it can be split into a small square surrounded by four trapezoids.

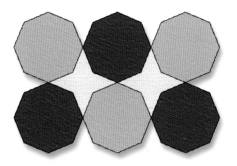

Stars with a square and four trapezoids

It is possible to begin the star with the square, then pick up the stitches for the trapezoid, but the easier way of getting the correct size is to make the pieces separately and stitch them together.

- Make the four trapezoids first.
- Use your calculations for the octagon.
- The straight sides will be **a** ridges, the width will be **a/1.4**.
- Make a slip knot and knit into it twice.
- **Next row:** knit.
- **Next row:** knit to the last stitch; knit into the last stitch twice.
- Repeat these two rows until you have **a/1.4** stitches.
- Knit straight until the total number of ridges is **a**. Bind off loosely.
- Stitch the four trapezoids as shown on the completed star, matching ridges from one with stitches from the next.
- Knit a small basic square to fit the remaining hole. Sew in place.

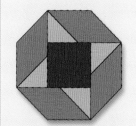

Note

Octagons cover more space when joined point-to-point. The width from point-to-point is 2.6 times the length of one side.

Making octagons from shapes

The octagons can be made up from combinations of other shapes.

A square surrounded by rectangles and triangles.

This large square touches the edges of the octagon. The extra shapes are trapezoids.

A square, four triangles, and four lozenges give the impression of a rotating star within an octagon.

Alternative ways of creating squares

The method you have learned for making a square is probably the easiest, especially for a beginner, but it certainly isn't the only way.

Using the same basic method, there are many ways of increasing and decreasing at the beginning or end of rows. A good knitting "encyclopedia" will show you lots of methods you might like to try, including slightly holey, lacy edges.

Some people dislike constantly turning the work when making small pieces. Using very short needles sometimes helps. Cut down a longer pair of needles, if necessary. Another solution is to learn to knit backward so you never need to turn the work.

Square on double-pointed needles

1 Working in rounds, knitting every round does not result in garter stitch. It creates stockinette stitch and the proportions of the stitches will not be the same. The square will quickly stop lying flat. If you want to try it, you will need extra increases.

2 You can work around and around if you knit one round and purl the next. The result will be garter stitch.

3 Cast on eight stitches and join them into a ring. If using double-pointed needles, put two stitches on each of four needles and knit with a fifth. Increase at both ends of each needle until the square is the size you want. If working on circular needles, divide the stitches with markers.

Other ways to create a square

Straight square

▪ Cast on the number of stitches you need.
▪ Knit straight for the same number of garter ridges.
▪ Bind off.
   For this method, you need to know the gauge that will give you the right size square before you begin.

Magic or mitered squares

There are many books available where mitered squares are explained in detail. They can be knitted from the outside in or from the center. Starting at the outside reveals the magic of the squares as a straight row of knitting gradually turns into a square. It is also very easy to connect squares together by picking up stitches from one to start the next. Starting from the center has the advantage that you can adjust the size without having worked out your gauge first.

From the outside in

1 Cast on an even number of stitches and put a marker between the two center stitches.

2 **Row 1**: knit, knitting two together at each side of the marker.
Row 2: knit. Repeat these two rows until two stitches are left. Knit two together and bind off.

From the center out

1 Cast on two stitches and put a marker between them. Knit every row, increasing in the stitch immediately before the marker.

2 Continue in this way until the square is the size you want. Bind off loosely, or keep the stitches on a spare needle if you intend to knit another shape directly onto them.

Raised shapes

You will want to produce a tidy outline shape to fit your overall plan for the item you are making (see pages 64–67), but within that outline you can add raised shapes.

If the shape stands out too far from the background, it may sag and get pushed around as you wear your garment. The tighter you knit, the less likely this is to happen.

Generally, the shapes need to be surrounded and supported by some firm, flat shapes. In order to decide how to make these raised surfaces, it is best to think of the hole you need to fill and what the outside of it looks like.

Creating raised shapes

Make a raised shape using different thicknesses of yarn

1 Using bulky yarn, cast on 10 stitches and knit a triangle that is straight on one side and sloping at 45 degrees at the others. This triangle will be more flexible if you knit quite loosely.

Using a thinner yarn, pick up 14 stitches along the sloping edge. Next row: knit to last stitch; knit twice into last stitch. Repeat until you have 20 stitches. Next row: knit to last two stitches; knit two together. Repeat until all stitches are worked off.

2 Using a thinner yarn, pick up 10 stitches from the cast-on stitches of the triangle and 7 stitches from the shorter edge of shape 2 (17 stitches total). Knit straight for 4½ ridges. Bind off loosely on the wrong side.

3 Using thinner yarn, pick up 7 stitches from the other short edge of shape 2, 10 stitches from the ends of the ridges of shape 1, and 5 stitches from the ends of the ridges of shape 3 (22 stitches). Knit straight for 4½ ridges. Bind off loosely on the wrong side.

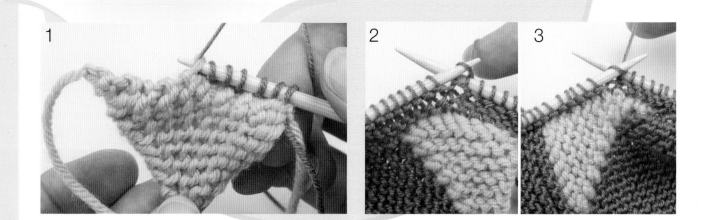

Other ways to create raised shapes

There are many other ways to make raised shapes. Here are two ideas for distorting the surface within a shape.

Irregular shaping

1 Knit backward and forward at random.

2 Knit a few stitches. Turn. Knit back a few stitches. Turn. Repeat this process as often as you want. Whenever you decide to knit to the edge of the shape, remember to do the normal shaping.

More regular shaping

1 Knit twice into some of the stitches. Knit straight on the next row. On the next row either increase again or decrease, depending on the effect you want to create.

2 The effects will differ according to your yarn and the size of the shape you are making. Experimentation is the best way to find an effect you like.

Tips for raised shapes

- Always knit at least two rows at the start, with only the normal shaping.

- Never use the first two or last two stitches as part of the distortion.

- Never have fewer stitches than you would have in the "normal" shape.

- Whenever you reach the edge of the shape, remember to do the normal shaping.

1

2

1

2

Combining shapes to fit

In order to join shapes together around a point, all the angles of the corners must add up to 360 degrees. To keep things simple, all of the shapes used so far are made from 45-, 90-, and 135-degree angles. Shapes with these angles can be in any order around the point. It is worth thinking about this at an early stage in your design.

Joining the shapes around a point

Where shapes meet around a point, there can be a minimum of three shapes and a maximum of eight.

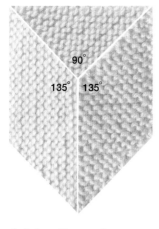

Joining three pieces together

If three shapes meet at a point, two of them must have 135-degree angles and the other one must be 90 degrees. No other combination will result in the 360 degrees needed to make a full circle around the point.

Joining four pieces together

There are three different possible combinations of angles when four shapes meet at a point.

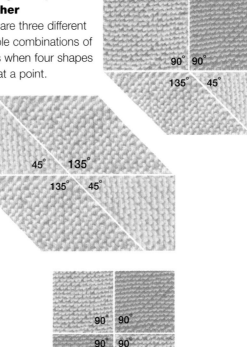

Joining five pieces together

There are two combinations using five shapes.

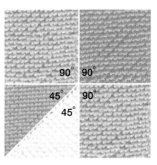

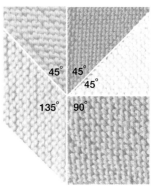

Joining six pieces together

There are two combinations of six shapes.

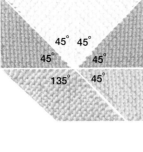

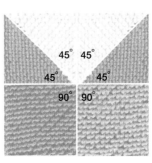

Joining seven or eight pieces together

There is only one possible combination each for joining seven and eight shapes.

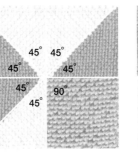

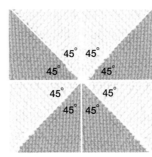

Using small shapes to make a block

Combine any small shapes to make a block. Ensure that the angles at each point add up to 360 degrees. Make several identical blocks and arrange them in different ways.

Swapping the order

There are many possibilities if you change the arrangement of the blocks and even more when you start to change the colors.

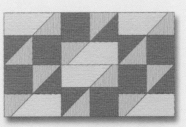

Turn individual blocks.

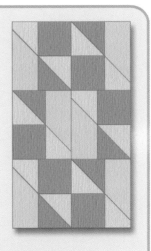

Turning the whole design on its side makes it look different again.

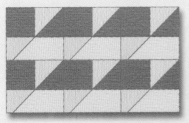

The block can be repeated with all blocks facing the same way . . .

. . . or some rows can be turned the opposite way.

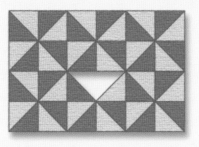

CHAPTER THREE

color and design

In this chapter...

Color

The use of color is a very personal choice. Everyone has likes and dislikes, often for reasons that can't be explained. A good way of choosing color combinations is to base them on something you have seen and liked. For instance, a peach or nectarine is not peach-colored. The skin can be made up of flecks of many shades ranging from pale orange to the deepest red. The colors work well in nature; they work equally well in yarns.

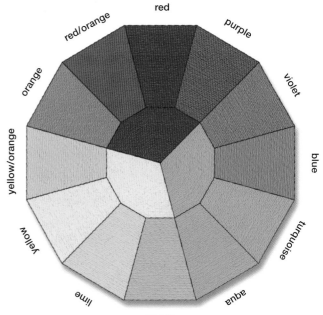

Choosing colors from pictures

If you don't see anything around you, look at the photographs in a magazine for inspiration. Make a small card frame and place it over different parts of the picture so that you are seeing only colors, not the subject. Cut out and keep any areas that appeal to you.

There will often be several very close shades in a chosen area and you might want to work with these, not just the obvious main colors. Use roughly the same proportion of each color in your item as there is in the picture.

There are a huge number of plain yarns available, even before you start to consider other variables such as thickness and fiber. Most yarn manufacturers produce shade cards.

▲ *The color wheel shown above is an arrangement of colors that demonstrates the basic elements of color theory. This standard wheel displays the primary colors (red, yellow and blue) on the inside circle with secondary colors on the outside circle.*

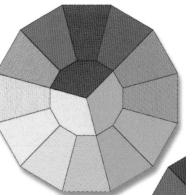

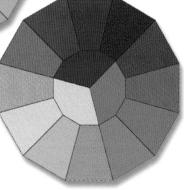

▲▶ *Choose colors from within the same palette. Shown above, a pastel palette, and right, a brighter palette.*

◀ *When looking in magazines for inspiration, use a card frame to isolate key colors.*

You can find every color in a wide range of shades and textures. Create your own shade card, or use the manufacturer's.

Same yarn, with direction changed.

Different yarns from the same manufacturer.

Assorted yarns provide contrast.

Using the same yarn

The same yarn worked in different directions usually looks as though you have used closely matched shades. The light is reflected at various angles to give different impressions. This is particularly true of textured stitches like garter stitch.

Using different types of yarn from the same manufacturer

Choose yarns from the same manufacturer in the same shade but different fibers. For example, a woollen yarn will look slightly different from a cotton yarn dyed with the same color, because the fibers absorb and reflect light differently. Some people might consider this to be a matter of texture, not coloring. It can be difficult to separate the two, but it really doesn't matter as long as you like the effect you get.

Using different types of yarn from different manufacturers

Combine yarns from various manufacturers. Many ranges of yarn change with fashion trends and you will find that manufacturers often include very similar colors. A good yarn shop will stock several ranges and you can mix and match from them.

Tips for combining yarn

■ Stick to standard thicknesses of yarn because the novelty yarns often work to a different gauge than others. You will not be able to create shapes in regular sizes when the yarns don't match.

■ When you wash your finished item, follow the instructions for the yarn that needs the most gentle treatment.

Pale green plus white.

Pale green plus silver.

Pale green plus gray.

Make your own subtle yarns

Use one basic yarn throughout and mix a variety of thinner yarns with it to change the overall appearance. There are so many possible combinations it is impossible to say what effect you will get in each case. It is a matter of experimentation.

A pale color needs very little extra color to change it. For example, if you are working with a pale green yarn and add a white yarn in some shapes, a silver-gray yarn in others and a darker gray in the rest, you will have three noticeably different shades. The added yarn can be of any thickness but it is best if it is thinner than the starting yarn. You must add a second strand to all shapes. Do not make any in the original yarn by itself. Treat the combined yarns as one.

Dark blue yarn mixed with three different reds will give three shades of purple in much the same way as mixing paint. Try twisting the yarns together to get an idea of the result.

Note

■ When you are assessing colors, half-close your eyes so you are seeing the overall effect. You will immediately spot anything that looks out of place. When you have mixed yarns, you will see a tweedy, flecked effect close-up and a more blended effect from further away. You don't have to be subtle!

Two swatches use the same shade of red, mixed with blues. Two use the same shade of blue; one mixed with the red, the other with brown.

Experimenting and using other colors

You will find many books about color in the arts and crafts sections of your library. It is not necessary to know, or use, the technical terms. Some people find them helpful; others prefer to work with what they already know. Everyone understands words such as light, dark, bright, dull, vibrant, and muted, and they are particularly easy to use as comparisons. We can all say whether one yarn is darker or paler than another without having to explain how or why. Use your own instincts.

If you are making garments for yourself, you know which colors suit you best. That doesn't mean you can't ever use other colors though—just use them in smaller amounts, away from your face.

Neutral colors

We tend to think of white/cream/beige shades as neutral, but these are often too insignificant and make a design look washed out. Very dark shades can also be considered to be neutral. The darkest shades of navy, brown, purple, or green are the perfect foil for many color schemes.

Harmonious effect

When you want colors to blend together, choose all pale, or all dark, or all bright, and so on. Alternatively, choose several shades from the same area of a color wheel. Squint at your chosen colors and reject any that stand out from the rest.

Contrasting colors

Choose contrasting colors to add vivacity and vibrancy to your design.

Harmonious effect, achieved by using complementary colors, gives a calm feel to the design.

Contrasting effect, producing a more vibrant feel.

The same shade of pink mixed with two different blues.

How many colors do you need?

The number of colors depends very much on your design and the effect you are trying to create. If the object is to color a pattern without any adjacent pieces being the same, you will never need more than four colors. Of course, you can choose to use more.

A checkerboard design needs only two colors.

A staggered design needs three.

Experiment with the colors you happen to have. You may be surprised by the results.

Four colors are needed for this complex design.

Arranging the colors

These strips show you some of the possibilities for arranging color. Unless you are knitting scarves, you are not likely to be making strips of squares.

When you have two colors, you can make two different patterns (although you might argue that this is the same pattern turned around).

When you add a third square, it can go behind, between, or in front of the existing squares, making a total of six possible combinations.

When a fourth color is added, it can go in any of four positions, in each of the six existing patterns—a total of twenty-four.

Again, you might see some of these combinations as being the same, but starting in a different place or going in the opposite direction. We all look at the world differently!

The same color in another place will vary the effect.

The appearance of a particular color is strongly affected by the colors around it. It can also be affected by the light. You should never take separate balls of yarn and assume that because you like them individually, you are certain to like them together. Look at them together, with eyes half-closed, under as many lighting conditions as possible. If you like the combination in all circumstances, you will almost certainly like the finished item.

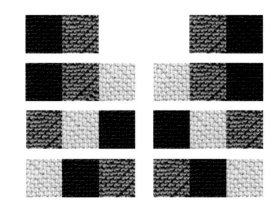

Working with two or three colors.

These are all the possible combinations of four colors arranged in a line.

Visual effects— optical illusions using color

These effects are all created by coloring the design in different ways. The flower design is probably seen in the same way by everyone, but all the others will be interpreted according to what the onlooker perceives them to be.

Optical illusions can easily be created in repeating patterns such as these. When looking at a darker shade, the eye may tell the brain that it is an area of shadow. A brighter shade could be one where the light is falling directly onto it. A pale shade could be a semi-shadow. Putting all this information together may give the illusion of boxes, steps, or houses. Merely changing the positions of two colors gives a new effect.

A multicolored random version gives the brain lots of conflicting information, which some people see as confusing, while others see it as exciting.

Visual effects—optical illusions using shape
It is easiest to create optical illusions with repeated motifs. They can confuse without giving the brain too much information at once.

Cubes?
These 4 sets of cubes (below) look very different.

Do you see cubes or a star?

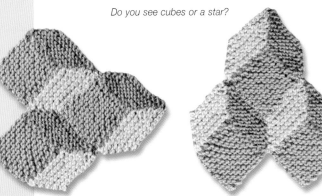

1 A set of 3 cubes, created by using lozenges to shadow squares.

2 The same set of cubes turned 90 degrees clockwise.

3 The same set of cubes, turned 180 degrees.

4 The same set of cubes, turned 90 degrees counterclockwise.

They are actually identical—the block has merely been turned around. Brown is always on top of, and below, the blue square. Cream is always to left and right. The position of the lightest shape suggests the direction of light on a cube.

Focus on looking at any one block and you will begin to see the cubes "move." Any colors could be used to create the cubes—the effect will always work. The colors determine how the brain sorts out the information it is receiving.

Now look at the larger pattern on the left, which is made up of the same colors used in a slightly more complex design. The squares no longer make such an obvious pattern—perhaps they are making two patterns at once, and some people see cubes while others see a star.

Squares?
Each square has a trapezoid on two of its sides, making a new square. When these new squares are put together, they begin to create the illusion of looking through a series of windows. Turning the shapes through 90 degrees changes the illusion slightly, as the windows appear to be pointing in a different direction.

These two blocks are identical but the relative position of the light squares to the other shapes changes the illusion.

Optical illusion designs

At the design stage (see pages 64–67), play around with colors within your design—there's an infinite array of effects you could achieve!

A two-color repeating windmill or cube pattern.

The same design in two different shades of the same color.

Highlight the windmills by working with one color per windmill.

Use a random color sequence to confuse the eye.

For a subtle effect, highlight just one element of the repeating pattern in a different color.

Create a chevron effect.

Create a wavy step effect by using 3 colors.

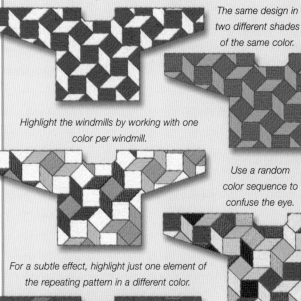

Using yarn with dramatic changes.

Using yarn with subtle changes.

Combining yarn and fabric.

Visual effects—mixed colors and textures

There are many multicolored yarns on the market. They come in many variations and are created by a variety of dyeing techniques. Some have very subtle color changes over a long length; some change color very frequently; some are bright; some are softly toning. You could even try mixing your own multicolored yarn!

Combining textured or flecked yarns

Textured yarns are available in all kinds of fibers. A smooth yarn is the perfect foil for some of the textures.

The simplest yarn with flecks of another color could be a good starting point. The flecks may be in a color you might not normally use, but if the combination of colors works in the yarn, it will also work if you pick out the second color for some of your other shapes.

Using yarn with subtle changes

Make your garment in one yarn that changes gradually and the shapes, knitted in different directions, may no longer be obvious, but the areas of color will produce a special effect of their own. Or try using a variegated yarn for some shapes and a contrasting solid for the rest.

Using yarn with dramatic changes

Using a brightly colored, frequently changing yarn could be too overwhelming to use for a whole garment, but could be wonderful if used for a few shapes surrounded by other solid-colored shapes, picking out the colors from the mixture.

Unconventional yarns

Texture can be far more than using a ready-made textured yarn. You can knit with anything that can be made into strands and is not sharp or dangerous. Perhaps you already have string or garden twine that is flexible enough to knit with, though it might be hard and should only be used for pieces that will not irritate the skin. You must remember to be especially careful when choosing yarn to create children's garments.

Self-striping yarns

Some yarns, like those intended for knitting socks, are self-striping. This only works if you have the correct number of stitches on each row—knitting to a different width will produce irregularly shaped areas of color. Allow shapes to evolve naturally. If you try to make them all the same, any that don't quite match will look wrong.

Combining yarn and fabric

Fabric shapes can be used to complement your knitted pieces. Cut the shape the same size as a knitted piece, then stitch all around the edges using a serger, or blanket-stitch by hand. Join to other shapes by picking up stitches from the loops of thread created by the serger. Very firm fabrics can have stitches picked up through holes punched at intervals.

What else is there?

Check a department store or craft shop for ribbon, lace, binding, or paper. Unless you can buy these on large rolls, they could be very expensive for making more than a few shapes.

Recycle plastic bags by cutting them into strips. Cut off the handles, then cut in a spiral using as much of the bag as possible. This yarn would probably be too hot and sticky for a sweater, but good for a hat, bag, or garden cushions. Plastic bags come in a huge range of colors and will cost you little or nothing.

Almost any fabric could be cut into strips. Some will fray, but you might like this effect. Very fine fabrics might look squashed when knitted and completely different from the starting fabric. Stretch fabrics can pull stitches very tight and be difficult to work with. Printed fabrics are often much paler on the back than on the front, and it is very difficult to always keep this side out of sight. Give life to old clothes by ripping the seams and using the fabric for yarn.

There are some fabrics specifically intended for other purposes that can be used to good effect, such as waterproof kite-making fabric or crunchy netting.

Knitting with plastic bags.

Knitting with recycled fabric.

How to recycle fabric

To get the maximum length either:
- Cut in a continuous spiral from one corner; or
- Fold the fabric in half, make cuts as shown, then cut across the fold on all sections except those at the end. You will have a huge loop that can be wound into a ball.

Practice the technique first with a small piece of paper.

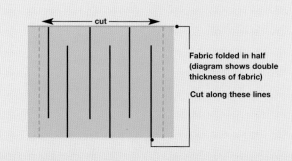

cut

Fabric folded in half (diagram shows double thickness of fabric)

Cut along these lines

Have you accidentally felted your favorite sweater?

Cut it into shapes and use it to make a new sweater. Use the paper template you had for your squares (or other shape) and cut shapes from your felted fabric. They should be exact size of the template. Do not allow for turning under or seaming.

Stitch around all edges of the shapes with a serger or zigzag sewing-machine.

If you do not have a sewing-machine, then blanket stitch the edges.

Blanket stitch around a fabric square, and then join to a knitted square.

Planning your design

The size of your new sweater, cardigan, or jacket might be very different from your actual measurements. Commercial patterns allow a certain amount of "ease." The amount can vary enormously between designs.

You will have to decide for yourself how much ease you need for your own design—but there is an easy way to do this.

Basic shape

The basic shape of the front and back will usually be a rectangle; however, there may be some shaping for the waist and chest, or a band at the bottom which has gathered the garment in. Try to establish the size of the key measurements shown on the diagram below by pulling the garment flat.
You don't have to take all the measurements from one garment. If the length, sleeves, etc. are not quite right, find other garments that are the size you want. Take the width from one, the length from another, and the sleeves from another to get your ideal shape.

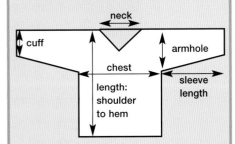

Taking measurements from an original garment

It doesn't matter whether you work in inches or centimeters, as long as you are consistent. Use a diagram, like the one below, to record your measurements.

Necklines vary a great deal and at this stage all you need to know is the size of the hole you want to leave. Ignore any collar or band, and measure the size of the neck you want from the main part of the garment.

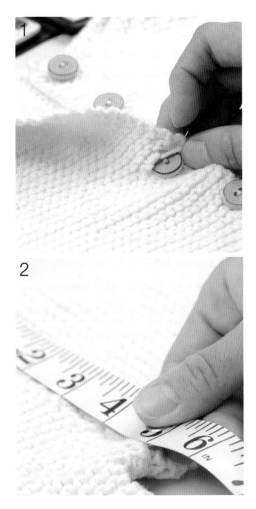

1 Find an old sweater or cardigan that fits widthwise the way you want your new garment to fit. It doesn't matter if it's a little too small, as you can adjust the measurements later. Lay this out on a flat surface, and fasten any zippers or buttons.

2 Measure the garment's width. If the garment you are measuring is also the correct length, or has the right-sized armholes, neck or sleeves, take these measurements too. You can take measurements from more than one garment, and use only the desired dimensions from each item. Sleeves and lower edges may have been gathered and these will have to be gently stretched to find the knitted dimensions, assuming you want the same amount of fullness.

3

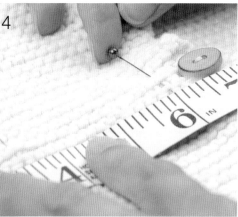

4

3 Make a note of these measurements onto a scale drawing. This will help you to put the measurements in context, and to work out how many shapes will fit into the garment's dimensions.

4 Working across the garment, pin out your initial ideas of how the shapes fit. It is a good idea to use the width as a guide as there is often more flexibility in the length, but if this is not the case, start with the most important dimension.

5 It is useful to bring together yarn samples, buttons, and even fabrics, so that you can find good yarns to fit your design. Knit some sample blocks and lay them out to gauge their effect.

Sizing your squares

Try different sizes of squares without having to knit them by simply dividing into the total number of stitches. The smaller the square, the greater the number of squares you will fit onto your garment.
The example below has 120 stitches across the width of the sweater. This total has been divided by convenient numbers to establish the best options for the sizes of the squares. Choosing a convenient measure makes it easier to check the depth and width of the individual blocks, and to press the pieces later.

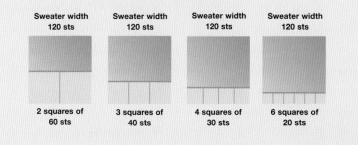

Sweater width 120 sts	Sweater width 120 sts	Sweater width 120 sts	Sweater width 120 sts
2 squares of 60 sts	3 squares of 40 sts	4 squares of 30 sts	6 squares of 20 sts

5

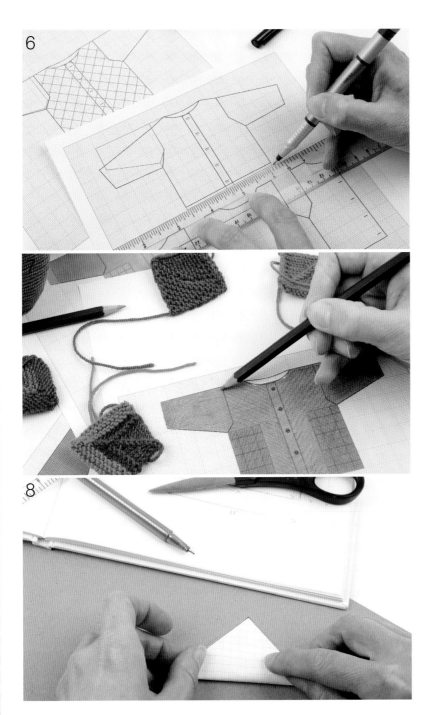

6 Once a basic unit or block size has been established, draw out the garment to scale on graph paper, simplify the angles to 45 and 90 degrees, and make any adjustments for ease or block size.

7 Make several copies of the drawing made on graph paper and draw various ideas over the top—experiment with color and geometric shapes. Knit sample blocks based on the basic unit you worked out previously.

Making paper templates

Once you are happy with the design, it is time to make paper templates. It is worth taking the time to make actual-size templates of all the major shapes in your design. This will allow you to check that they fit together to the correct size. Any fairly stiff paper can be used and squared paper will make the template easier to draw out.

8 Start with one of the more basic shapes whose width and depth can easily be marked on squared paper. Draw and cut out the shape. Not all the shapes need to be drawn out—sometimes folding existing templates can create another shape in the design.

Tip

A quilter's rule can be an aid to drawing templates on plain paper. The block divisions and marked angles make it possible to draw out complex shapes by positioning the ruler over lines already made.

9 If the template dimensions are based on convenient measurements, then simply make a note of stitch counts before increases and decreases. This can be done on the template.

10 Once the size of the first template has been established, draw the remaining shapes onto squared paper. Start with an adjacent shape and check any dimensions you can with a template or templates you have already made.

Bringing it together

Now is the time to get ready to start knitting. This is the most satisfying stage so far, as you start to see the garment take shape before your eyes. Remember that the best thing about no-pattern knits is the flexibility it affords—if something in your design looks as if it isn't working, simply amend your plan as you knit.

11 Draw out a knitting plan or diagram of the garment on graph paper. Make notes so you remember your decisions; these notes can be considered and developed as you knit, which will help with this garment and your next design. Make yourself a stencil of frequently used shapes.

12 Follow your knitting plan, but remember you are gaining experience about the yarn and the pattern as you knit. So, check and double-check crucial dimensions, and make any additional notes and adjustments as you go along.

Designing sleeves

The easiest way for a beginner to shape the edges of a sleeve is with wedge shapes made from rows of straight knitting. In the example shown here, the squares have a diagonal of 28 stitches, so the number of stitches to be picked up along the edge is 20.

1 Use a completed square or a template to measure the distance from the square to the edge of the sleeve at the top of the wedge. In this example, the extra piece needed is three-quarters of the square's width, so will need 15 ridges.

2 Measure the distance at the bottom of the wedge in the same way. Here, it is half the width of the square, so needs 10 ridges. This means that 15 ridges are needed at one end, but only 10 at the other, so 5 stitches must be lost evenly. The edge of the adjacent square is 20 stitches high. Divide the number of rows by the number of stitches you need to lose. In this case, 20 divided by 5 equals 4. This means that the stitches have to be in groups of 4.

3

3 Knit the 10 ridges that you need for all stitches, ending at the narrow end of the wedge. Turn and bind off 4 stitches. Knit to the wide end, then back towards the narrow end. Bind off 4 stitches at the start of every row at the narrow end, until all stitches have gone.

4 If the sleeve has the same slope all the way down, you will need to lose the same number of stitches on each wedge. Shaping will be the same, regardless of the size of the wedge. The top of one wedge will have the same number of ridges at its widest point as the one above had at its narrowest.

Alternative method
As an alternative, simple method, the pieces can be knitted parallel to the top and bottom of the square. In the example, you will need 15 stitches at the top of the larger wedge and 10 stitches at the bottom. Therefore, you need to lose 5 stitches in 20 ridges of knitting. Decrease one stitch at the end of every fourth ridge. Shape other wedges in the same way.

4

Tapered sleeves

Shape **1** is the same width as a square along the top edge, so (starting at the top left corner) the number of increases along the top edge will be the same as for the other squares. The other side of the shape does not spread out as much as for a square, so will need fewer increases. Shapes **2** and **3** have the slope going in the same direction but the top edges are very much smaller. Shape **4** is exactly the same as shape 1—it is one square wide at the top and has the same slope. Shape **5** has a complete half-square before you need to start the shaping. The shaped edge makes the shape less than a square, so the stitches need to disappear more quickly. Extra decreases will be needed. Shape **8** is identical to shape 5. Similar principles apply to shapes **6** and **7**.

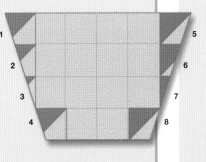

Edgings and bands

So far, you have learned the basics that you need to create your garment. However, to finish your garment to perfection, you will need to think about edgings, bands, buttonholes, trimmings, and necklines. These details will add another unique element to your design and you are still free to change your mind as you go along.

You could introduce some ribbing into edging modules to help grip.

Edgings

At the edges of your garment there is nothing to keep the edges in place, so you will usually need at least one row of extra knitting to prevent movement.

"Edgings" refers to the lower edges, sleeves or armholes, necklines, pockets, and openings of any other kind, in a garment. In cushions, bags, and afghans, it refers to any of the outside edges.

Wherever the edgings may be, the rules, for a straight edge, are the same. If you want the pieces to stay flat, pick up the same number of stitches across each shape as you would when adding another small shape.

Straight edges

If you want nothing more than an edge to keep the shapes firm, bind off knitwise on the next row. In order not to pull in the edge, make this bind off loose, possibly using a larger-size needle than you used for the knitting. You could use your preferred method of binding off.

For a wider flat band, knit as many rows of garter stitch as you need, then bind off as before. Straight edges work particularly well on blankets and cushions, although they can also be used to good effect on garments.

Button and buttonhole bands

These are no different from any other bands. Make these a little wider than the buttons. You do not have to space buttons evenly—they could line up with various parts of your design. Consider zippers, ties, snaps, and other fastenings instead of buttons.

- Work the button side first so that you can mark the places for the buttons. Make the buttonhole band to match, lining up the buttonholes with the marked positions.

- Knit to one stitch before the marked position, bind off 2 stitches and continue to next position. On the next row, cast on two above the bound-off stitches. For large buttons, you may need to bind off more stitches.

- For a child's garment, the button and buttonhole bands could be across the shoulders. This should be completed before the sleeves are made.

Tip

If you are making a wall-hanging, create a channel for a hanging pole by knitting the top edging twice as wide as the others. Fold over and stitch into place, leaving the ends open.

Flared edges

Edgings don't have to pull inwards and hold the garment to your shape. They can be decorative and flare out, such as on the hat shown below. This can also be used on the bottom edge or collar of a sweater.

Pick up the number of stitches you need in the normal way and knit at least one row even. Knit more than one row even

for a narrow flat band before the start of the flare.

Increasing makes the band flare. (See page 18 for instructions.) Note that when all increases go in the same direction, the band may appear to twist.

Increases in the same place on successive rows will result in small points. This could be a design feature, but avoid increasing in the same place if you want a softer flare.

Fitted bands

The bottom edges of your sweater may need a fitted band. Garter stitch does not grip as well as a rib would, so take care to make the band the actual size required.

To work out the number of stitches, measure your hips or wrists and work out how many of your starting squares would fit into this measurement. Multiply the number of squares by the

number of stitches needed at the edge of one square. Pick up this total number of stitches, distributing them proportionally across the shapes.

If your band has far fewer stitches than the bottom edge of your shapes, pick up twice as many stitches as you calculated, then knit two together all across the next row. This will make a smoother fit.

Embellishing your edgings

To pull a garment together and add flair, try adding beads into your design, as shown on the hat below. Other ideas include using a lacy trim, tassels, or pompoms. Refer to a good knitting encyclopedia for new ideas.

See also Embellishments on pages 84–91

Necklines and collars

Some of your designs will need nothing more than one row of knitting to hold all the edges in place, but generally your garments will benefit from a simple neckline or collar. There are three simple neckline shapes—square, V-neck, and round. Once you know how to create these, you can adapt them to fit any of your designs.

Drawing your neckline on a grid

As for the sleeve, the easiest way to design a collar is to create a template of the shape you want. This can be based either on a garment you already have, or on draping fabric around your shoulders and cutting it to shape. Unfortunately because the shape of the neckline will determine the shape of the collar, this decision cannot be entirely left until the body of the garment has been completed. The following are only suggestions—there are many more possibilities.

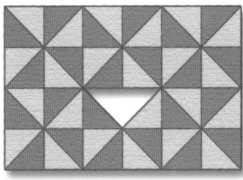
V-neck follows the pattern in the squares.

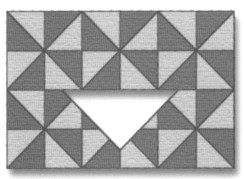
A larger V-neck cuts across some shapes.

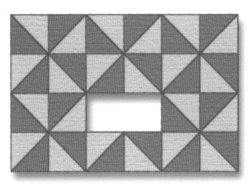
Rectangle follows lines of squares.

A large rectangular neckline cuts across some shapes. All edges are parallel to the sides or top and bottom.

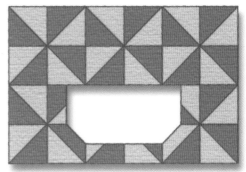
A series of short straight edges will distort into a curve without any noticeable effect on the overall design.

1. RUFFLE COLLAR This collar can be added to most neckline shapes. Measure around the neckline, including any facings. Divide this evenly into convenient lengths. Knit a rectangle whose shorter edge is the same depth as the desired ruffle and longer edge matches the divided length. Then knit the first half of a basic square to create a right-angle triangle until the edges match that of ruffle depth. Knit alternate rectangles and triangles, joining them as you knit, until the desired length is reached. Stitch the collar in place.

2. OFF-THE-SHOULDER COLLAR Measure and divide the neckline as for the polo neck, but knit a trapezoid starting at the 90-degree point instead of a rectangle. The width matches the divided length and will attach to the neckline; the longest edge is the depth of the collar. Sew together as mirrored pairs and attach to the neckline. Keep the points as a feature or knit right-angle triangles to fill the gaps.

6. POLO NECKS This collar is usually added to a rounded neckline. Start by measuring around the neckline and dividing the distance evenly by a number that can be divided by two and about 1½ inches (3.7 cm) wide. Knit a rectangle whose shorter edge matches the divided length and the longest edge is the depth of the collar. Sew together as mirrored pairs and attach to the neckline. See also off-the-shoulder collar.

3. SIMPLE EDGING This edging can act as a collar on most necklines. Pick up stitches along the neckline, using the table on page 24 as a guide, and knit one, two or more rows back and forth or around and around before binding off. If applied to a v-neck, knit two stitches together at the point of the v.

5. PETER PAN COLLAR This collar is usually added to a round neckline. Cast on enough stitches for approximately half the collar depth. Knit, increasing into the last stitch of each row, until the number of ridges knitted equals the number of stitches cast on divided by 1.4. Knit without shaping until the edges equal that of half the neckline. Bind off. Make a second collar piece. Without joining the collar pieces together, stitch them in place. There will be a v-shaped gap at the center back.

4. SHAWL COLLAR This collar is usually added to a v-neckline. Knit a trapezoid starting at the 90-degree point, increasing at both edges until the width is the desired depth of the collar. Then continue as directed on page 38 until the shorter edge equals half the neckline measurement. Bind off. Make a second collar piece. Join the two pieces together along the shortest edges with the points to the outside. Stitch the collar in place.

Pockets

Pockets can be added anywhere that you can leave a shape unstitched or can apply a patch. There are two types of pocket: the inset pocket that lies behind the knitted fabric, and the patch pocket, which is applied to the surface of the fabric. Functional pockets should be larger than your hand and positioned within comfortable reach, but decorative pockets can be smaller. It is best to plan for pockets at the design stage, although patch pockets can be added later.

Tip

If the outer edge of a pocket opening shows any signs of stretching out of shape, pick up a row of stitches (following the usual rules) and bind off again, knitwise, on the next row.

Patch pockets

Patch pockets should be decorative as they will be in full view. They can be added as an afterthought by either making another shape (or shapes), matching the shapes on the garment or by knitting a contrasting shape or rectangle. The new shape can be sewn on top of the old, leaving one side open for access. Patch pockets can also be planned at the start and knitted with the other shapes.

Stitching patch pockets onto a garment

Attach a pocket by using mattress stitch. For added strength, the bottom of this pocket has been attached to the backing by picking up stitches on both pieces and binding them off on the wrong side.

Knitting patch pockets into a garment

1 Knit the front pocket shape and the backing as two separate pieces. Do not be tempted to knit them as one and fold them, as the fold will add bulk to the pocket.

2 Hold the two pieces together and pick up stitches through both layers. Knit the new shape as usual. These pockets are very firmly attached and become an integral part of the design, so cannot be removed later.

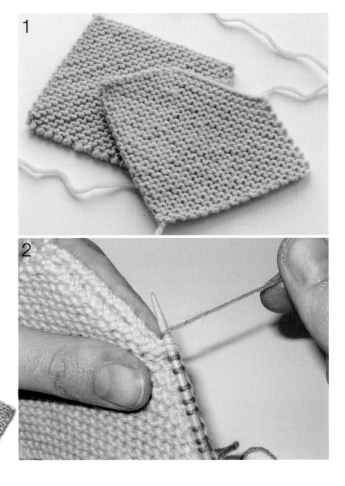

74

Decorative patch pockets

These two small pockets appear to sit on the surface of the fabric, but they are added at the original construction stage by knitting them into the garment. They show identical pockets added in different ways. Patch pockets look best when applied in pairs to a garment.

The pocket and backing have ridges going at 90 degrees to each other. The shapes are the same as those in the example opposite.

The pocket and backing have ridges going in the same direction as each other, which makes the pocket less conspicuous.

Inset pockets

If you don't wish to make a feature of the pocket, then knit an inset pocket, which can be made to be almost invisible. The opening can appear between two shapes or it can be created within a shape. For an opening between two shapes, simply leave the shapes either entirely or partially unattached. If the opening must appear within a shape, make sure the shape is big enough to have a margin of stitches about 1 inch (2.5 cm) on either side of the opening.

Work to the position of the opening, knit the required number of stitches across the top of the pocket, place them onto a stitch holder, and continue to the end of the row. On the next row, work to the position of the opening and cast the same number of stitches as were put onto the stitch holder. The stitches on the stitch holder can later be knitted or bound off.

A pocket has been inset behind the blue trapezoid. The top layer is incomplete so that the pocket can be seen. The finished pocket would be completely hidden, as the top edge would be finished in the tan yarn.

Create a pocket either by knitting an extra shape large enough to lie behind the opening, or by picking up stitches along the cast-on edge and knitting these stitches down to make the back of the pocket. The backing will not be seen, so it can be any color that will not show through the garment. Catch the pocket backing to the inside of the garment through the ridges or garter stitches. Take care not to let the stitches show on the outside.

Developing ideas

Now that you know the basic methods, don't restrict yourself to sweaters—adapt the ideas to make anything. Create a patchwork of modules to make a blanket; use scraps of yarn to make toys for a baby; or design a bag to go with your favorite outfit. Keep in mind the principles of no-pattern knits, but let your imagination run wild!

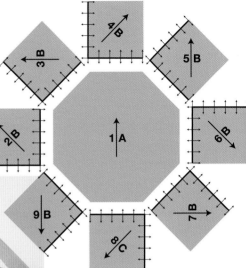

To match your sweater you could make a hat with eight squares (or more complex shapes) attached to an octagon. You don't even need to do any measuring.

Method for basic hat

1 Take a strip of gummed paper, wrap it tightly around your head, and cut it to the size of your head. (It is easier to have a friend do this for you.)

2 Cut the strip exactly in half and throw one half away.

3 Cut the other half exactly into four and stick these four pieces on a sheet of paper to form a square.

4 Use the square you have created as your template.

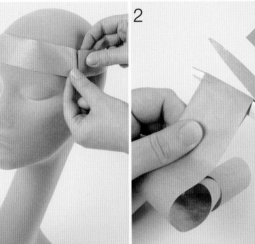

5 Increase as for the first half of a square until the work fits across the diagonal inside the square. You must make a note of the number of stitches. Complete by decreasing for second half of the square. Eight squares like this will join together to go around your head.

6 Make the top of the hat as explained in making an octagon (see page 44) and stitch the pieces together.

7 Add a band to stop the edge from stretching. Thread shirring elastic through the edge if necessary.

The lurex beaded (lurex with beads) hat was started with an octagon and the sides were knitted straight to form a head-hugger. The beads were threaded onto the yarn and a simple crochet chain was added attaching it to every third stitch of the hat, with the beads hanging in the loops.

Hat variations

Use a basic octagon shape, and then simply remember that the distance around the edges of the octagon needs 8 times as many stitches as one edge of the octagon. This number of stitches can be picked up and knitted downwards, or, the same number of garter stitch ridges will fit around the hat. Experiment with shapes and finishing effects and you'll be surprised how many different looks you can achieve.

Add beads to define the edges of the shapes used.

Knit the squares in different directions and add a small brim. Pick up the correct number of stitches. Increase at the corner of each square on alternate rows.

▼ Bags

You can't have enough bags. Just one color or texture can link one to a sweater or scarf to make an ensemble. Bags come in all shapes and sizes and a trip to a department store will fuel your imagination. One bag was inspired by a corded quilt pattern and the second by a Japanese purse in a local decorative arts museum. Finding the perfect button looked as if it was going to be a major problem and the idea of painting a perfectly shaped button seemed to be the solution.

Tip

A wooden button will absorb any pigment from a marker pen and will not necessarily need to be varnished. It may fade but then you just quickly paint it again.

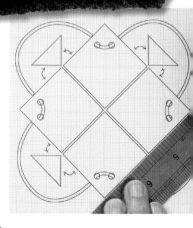

◄ Cushion

This is my favorite design for a cushion. It is just one of a thousand block designs that can be found in patchwork or math books. They can be used as single blocks or as part of a design of one or more blocks. It is a good idea is to draw and cut out smaller versions of the blocks you think you might use to try out some ideas.

Tip

The secret of making a good cushion is to use a filling slightly larger than the cover so that the cushion is well rounded.

► Shawl

Shawls and ponchos are perfect for trying out your own designs because they don't have to fit in the way a sweater does. Be as traditional or eccentric as you wish.

Useful information

The US government periodically produces statistics on the average sizes and proportions of the populace. Knitting and sewing patterns will also give you a good idea of sizing, but these figures should only be a guide and used when you can't get measurements for the person you wish to knit for.

The average head circumference for a:
baby—15 in. (38 cm)
12-year-old—18 in. (45 cm)
woman—20 in. (50 cm)
man—22 in. (55 cm)

The average foot length for a:
newborn—3¾ in. (9 cm)
6 months—4 in. (10 cm)
1 year—4½ in. (11.5 cm)

See the statistics from the US Bureau of Standards for more details.

▼ Scarf

Scarves are a great vehicle for trying out new ideas and color schemes. A math book and a childhood obsession with the graphic artist Escher inspired this scarf. As you can see from the work sheet, using the scarf flat was a happy accident; initially it was intended to resemble a chain of paper lanterns. Maybe that idea will still see the light of day.

▶ Mittens

Rather than knitting the thumb separately, it is possible to knit a mitten in two pieces with a seam around the top and sides of the hand. Maybe next time a cuff of rib will be used to help keep them on and keep out the cold. To make a custom pair of mittens, draw around your hand on squared paper and adjust the shapes so an outline is made up of angles of 45 or 90 degrees. Do not make the shape any bigger than your hand. The mittens will stretch to fit.

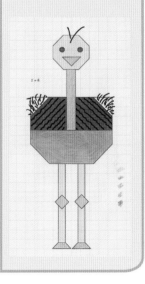

Alternative ideas

You can make literally anything as a modular toy—if the child you are knitting for has a passion for dinosaurs, trains, or birds, try breaking down the overall sketch into shapes that you can knit and then join together. Squared paper is helpful for this.

▼Toys

Children's toys are the perfect excuse to use your imagination. They allow artistic license and need not resemble anything known to man. Remember that safety is vital. Do not use toxic substances and secure elements firmly using strong materials. And, if we are talking of a wish list, being washable is useful, although felted wool has its own attraction. Try making this caterpillar from a string of octagons.

Modules for babies and toddlers

The two main advantages of this method of knitting are that you can make a garment any size you want, and that there are none of the usual seams to cause any irritation. These make it ideal for even the smallest baby garment. If you need to make a cardigan for a premature baby with a 12-inch (30-cm) chest, the planning is the same but there will be fewer shapes to make.

To avoid bulk, consider using finer yarns for a baby than you would for an adult. The rules remain the same whatever the size of the shapes and the thickness of the yarn.

Because baby items are so small, using a lot of different shapes might make the garment look too busy. A repeating, or symmetrical, design is often best.

These diagrams show the layouts for some of the effects you could achieve using simple, diagonally divided squares. They also show what you would see once the front and back were joined. Bands and edgings can be added later.

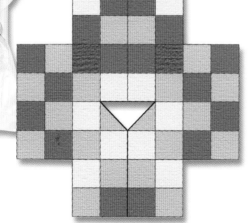

▲ Use odds and ends of yarn to create a lovely baby cardigan, and embellish with flat buttons.

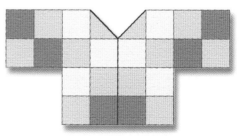

▼ Very small amounts of yarn are needed for the squares of a baby cardigan.

▲ Patterned squares look just as good on baby clothes as they do on adult-size items, but remember to use smaller squares for baby garments!

▼ Use cuddly yarn and more squares to make a sweater for an older child. This is essentially the same design as the pastel baby version above.

Getting garments to fit children

■ If you are making clothes for a child, it is probably best to make the new garment slightly bigger than the old favorite. Children tend to grow in length more quickly than they grow in width. A little extra length may be all you need for the body. Arms generally grow in proportion to height, so add a little to the sleeve length as well.

■ Modular garments are ideal for children since you can add more modules to lengthen the garments at a later date.

■ Children's heads are very large in relation to their bodies. A larger neckline is always necessary for a child when knitting a sweater. You can achieve this in a variety of ways, from using a wide boatline shape to having an opening that closes with buttons or a zipper. The neck is in proportion to the body, so the neckline of a jacket or cardigan can be close fitting.

See also Embellishments, pages 84–91

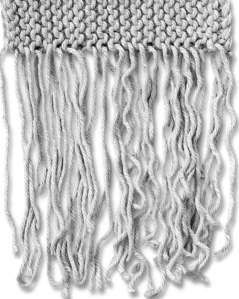

Embellishments

There are many ways to add extra interest, either during construction or afterward. Whether you need to insert buttonholes or want to add embellishments such as fringe, tassels, loops, i-cords, or pom-poms for that final touch, here are some simple techniques that require only small amounts of yarn.

Fringe

A fringe can add a wonderful finishing touch to the edge of a garment. A fringe looks lovely when added to the edge of a collar, and can be embellished further by adding beads.

Knitted fringe

This fringe is sewn on once the knitted piece is completed and is worked in garter stitch.

1 Cast on the number of stitches that, when knitted, make approximately one-fifth the length of the required fringe. Work in garter stitch until the band is the required length. Bind off the first four or five stitches.

2 Unravel the remaining stitches to create the fringe. This may be left as loops or trimmed.

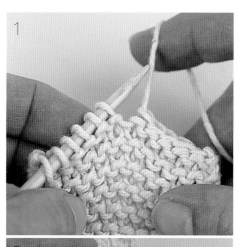

▲ A knitted fringe can be the perfect finishing touch.

Tip

■ A few yarns do not lend themselves to tassels or fringe. Slippery yarns may not stay in place, heavily textured yarns might be difficult to pull through, and some yarns will start to unravel.

▼ The fringe here consists of one strand knotted through the end of every garter stitch ridge. Use more strands or other spacing for a different effect.

Tassels

You will need a piece of cardboard, scissors, and a tapestry needle.

2 Cut the yarn, leaving a tail of about 10 inches (25 cm) and thread this tail into the needle.

3 Slip the yarn off the cardboard and wind the tail tightly around it, about ¹/₂ inch (¹/₂ cm) from one end. Bind tightly with several turns.

4 Slip the needle underneath the turns and bring it out at the top.

5 Pass the needle through all the small loops at the top of the tassel.

6 Knot the tail tightly at the top of the loop. Don't cut it off.

7 Cut through all of the strands at the bottom of the tassel, and trim to ensure that all are even.

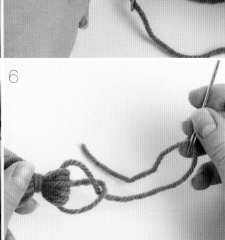

1 Decide how long you want the tassel to be. Cut a piece of cardboard about ¹/₂ inch (1.2 cm) wider than this measurement. Wind the yarn around the cardboard as many times as you want.

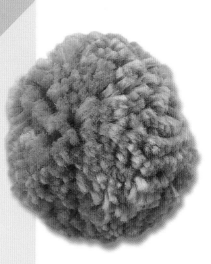

Pom-poms

Pom-pom making is a popular pastime for small children and is a great way to introduce them to yarns and the concept of knitting. Pom-poms can look lovely hanging from shelves or a Christmas tree, and are particularly attractive on cushions and winter hats. You can buy a ready-made pom-pom maker, but circles of cardboard work just as well. Cut two circles bigger than the required diameter of the pom-pom, with a smaller hole at the center.

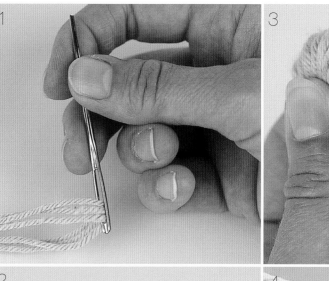

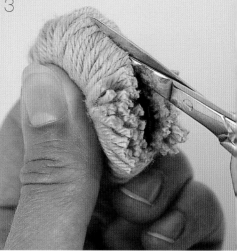

1 Thread a large sewing needle or bodkin with as many ends of yarn as it will take. The yarn ends should be approximately 3 feet (1 m) long.

2 Hold the two discs of the pom-pom maker together and thread the needle through the center, around the outside and back through the center from the front, holding the tail end of yarn in place with your thumb if need be. Continue to do this until the center hole is full.

3 Using a sharp pair of scissors, cut around the pom-pom, between the discs.

4 Tie a piece of yarn or sewing cotton around the center of the pom-pom as tightly as possible and remove the discs. Trim the pom-pom to form a ball.

Loops

Loops can be functional, used as buttonholes, or used simply as decoration. Either way, they are an easy way to add flair.

Sewn buttonhole loop

Sewn buttonhole loops are very effective when used for buttons that have a shank. They are made by sewing around a small loop of yarn.

1 Mark the position of the buttonhole using pins.Thread a large needle with the yarn and make a loop by bringing the yarn through the knitted piece from back to front and in by one stitch at the first pin.

2 Take the yarn back through the work at the second pin and then through near the first pin for a second time. Work buttonhole or blanket stitch around the loop until complete.

Loopy trim

A knitted, loopy trim works only in small areas, since it may distort the shape.

1 To work the loops, knit into the stitch in the normal way but do not let it slip off the left-hand needle.

2 Bring the yarn to the front and wrap a loop round your thumb close to the needle, take the yarn to the back and knit into the back of the stitch you kept on the needle. Repeat in every stitch.

i-cord

This cord is a knitted tube, useful for ties and handles. You will need two double-pointed needles, two or three sizes smaller than the size recommended for your yarn.

1 Cast on 3, 4, or 5 stitches. Knit one row in the usual way.

2 Without turning the work around, pass the needle with the stitches to your left hand. Push the stitches along to the right end of the needle. Pass the

yarn across the back of the stitches and pull tight to bunch the stitches together. Use the empty needle to knit another row from right to left.

3 Repeat to the length required. The knitting forms a small tube.

Adding beads

Beads can be used in many different ways and can be applied as the knitting is progressing or added later.

▲ Highlight the different directions of knitting by adding beads along the diagonal of your squares.

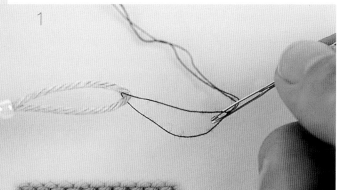

Adding beads while knitting

1 To add beads while knitting, thread them onto your yarn before you begin. Keep pushing them down out of the way until you reach the place where you want to attach a bead.

2 Slide the bead as close as you can to the knitting and work a very tight stitch, then continue as normal.

All beads, and other trims, must be washable if they are knitted into the design as it will not be possible to remove them. Also be aware that extra weight can distort the precision of your shapes. Use beads to define lines in your shapes or to add any pattern you want. Sequins could be used in the same way, but must have holes big enough to thread them onto the yarn.

▶ Use coordinating beads at the corners of squares.

Attaching by sewing

If you are unsure about the positioning of beads, wait until the item is complete before making a decision. Stitching them on is a long process, but they can be more easily removed this way.

A simple checkerboard pattern is enhanced by beads to tone with both colors. Use them at the corners or seams between shapes, in the middle of shapes, or hanging down to create a fringed effect.

To make the beads hang down in this way, a tiny gold ring was used beneath each bead. Using a sewing needle small enough to go through your beads, fasten the yarn securely on the back side of the knitted item, bring it to the front, pass the needle through the bead, through the ring, and up through the bead before fastening off.

Holes and spaces

Holes and spaces in your knitted pieces can create an attractive pattern. You could leave small spaces between shapes and fill them in some other way. (Large holes might allow the garment to stretch.) You could line your garment with a contrasting lining and the color will show through the holes.

Knitted holes

Small holes can be used to make patterns within a shape. Choose the spacing according to the pattern you want to make. If you can't visualize it, draw your shape on squared paper, using one square per stitch. Color the squares that will be holes.

1 Make the holes by your preferred method. A hole is created by knitting two stitches together, followed by bringing the yarn forward or around the needle to create a new stitch and maintain the same number of stitches.

2 The two stitches knitted together must include the one that is to be the hole. If it is the first of the two stitches, make the extra stitch in front of it. If it is the second stitch, make the extra stitch after it.

Holes should be used in moderation as too many will cause a shape to stretch.

▼ Sew around the edge of a small curtain ring using buttonhole or blanket stitch, and then use the covered ring to support the structure of a larger hole.

Crocheted holes

This is a small crochet square surrounded by garter stitch to make it the right size to fit with other shapes. The square consists of alternate trebles and chains. Two stitches were picked up from the edge of each square.

Any ready-made fabric with holes can be used in a similar way. Look for curtain nets or any other mesh fabric. A very small length of an exotic gold or silver mesh can provide the center for many shapes. Picking up stitches from any fabric will be a trial-and-error process until the work lies flat. One favorite is sequin waste (the strip that is left when sequins are punched out), although it is difficult to work with because the rows of holes form 60-degree angles. Stitches can be picked up easily from one pair of edges, but need to zigzag on the other edges.

Stitch patterns

Other stitches, such as stockinette, can be used inside the garter stitch shapes to create textured effects. Remember that the gauge of stockinette stitch, and other variations, is different from garter stitch, so you will need to keep this in mind when you knit. In both of these blocks, stockinette stitch has been used within a garter stitch "frame" to create an interesting visual effect. Using an alternative stitch within a garter stitch shape should enable you to easily retain your original shape.

3-D embellishment

Finish a shape in the usual way, then add another shape, wherever you want, by picking up another set of stitches along any vertical or horizontal line of bumps and working as for other shapes. One side will show bumps of the wrong color where you have picked up stitches. Make sure this is on the side that is to be out of sight.

This two-color square had another row of stitches picked up along the color change row. The third triangle is the same size as the underlying triangle.

Weaving

One of the delights of garter stitch is that the stitches are evenly spaced, obvious, and easy to count. This makes it ideal for adding yarn as an embellishment. This weaving is a plain dark square with two colors of yarn woven under alternate bumps of garter stitch. The yarn was used double. There are many ways to vary this technique:

■ Work the lines at any angle by counting across and up in a regular pattern.
■ Take the yarn to the back and bring up again where required. In a two-color design, use the same two colors for the weaving.
■ Use novelty yarns—only small quantities are needed. Weaving will not distort your shape but could add noticeably to the weight of the garment if there is a lot of it.

Parallelograms

The parallelograms for the base of this shape are alternately blue and pink. Stitches were picked up along the color change and the new parallelograms were knitted so they slope in the opposite direction. This creates an unusual visual effect, confusing the brain.

Experiment with adding new shapes on top of the old. If you don't like them, pull them out and no damage will have been done.

Embroidery

Many pieces can be enhanced with the addition of a little embroidery. Try adding a simple motif or monogram on a few shapes, or use embroidered buttons.

Dorset buttons

Dorset buttons can be made in almost endless permutations of color or just one color. Dorset buttons are especially effective on cushions and garments that require larger buttons since small ones can be tricky to make.

1 Using a long length of yarn, sew around the edge of a small curtain ring using buttonhole or blanket stitch. Holding the tail end of the yarn close to the ring, sew around both the ring and the tail until it has disappeared. Secure once the ring is full and turn the hem edge of the blanket stitch to the inside of the ring.

2 Using a second yarn, sew around the ring to create a web effect. Using two or three stitches, overcast the center of the spokes and secure the yarn.

3 Using a third yarn, thread the needle through from the back to the front of the button, close to the center of the web, between two spokes. Fill in the ring's center by working backstitch around the spokes. Bind off the yarn.

Embroidered buttons

You can buy button kits that consist of a two-part button: one side acts as the front, and the other side has a slot that holds the shank in place. Fabric is placed over the front of the button and clipped into place with the second piece.

Monogram

The monogram below is embroidered in chain stitch, using a smooth cotton yarn. Use any yarn, any stitches, and any design. The squareness of garter stitch makes it ideal for cross-stitch patterns. Embroidery will not distort the shapes.

CHAPTER FOUR

projects

In this chapter...

KEY

❷ = Degree of difficulty on a scale of 1–3

Booties

These booties use so little yarn that an investment in luxury yarns such as cashmere and silk will make them a joy to knit. Even with a strenuous laundry regime, they will last as long as they will fit the baby.

Template

Use this template to check the size of blocks A, B, C, and D.

For the suggested yarns, the number of stitches on the needle before decreasing should be: 17 stitches for blocks A, B, C, and D.

Blocks

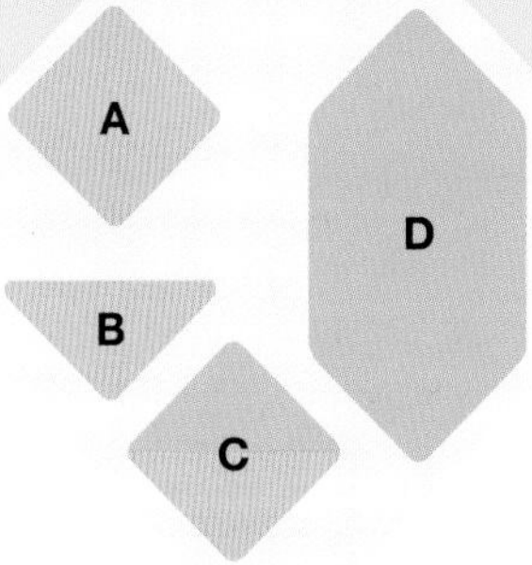

A

D

B

C

Size

0–3 months
To adjust the size, photocopy the template to the width of the foot plus ¼ inch (6 mm) on each side.

Materials

- For each of the two colors:
  ½ oz. (15 g) of fingering-weight yarn.
- A firm but soft gauge is required.

For the booties shown:

Rowan cashcotton 4-ply 1¾ oz. (50 g) balls

pink	1
green	1

- A selection of ribbons, buttons, and embroidery silks to embellish the booties.
- 1 pair of US 5 (3.75 mm) needles.

Blocks

Each bootie is made up of four different blocks, one of which is a basic square.

Block A is a basic square; see page 20.

Make a slip knot and increase at the end of every row until the sides of the square match the template (left). Work one row with no increases. Knit two stitches together at the end of every row until no stitches remain.

Block B is half a basic square, or a right-angle triangle; see page 32. Make a slip knot and increase at the end of every row until the sides of the square match the template.
Bind off.

Block C is a two-color basic square with eyelets. Make a slip knot and increase at the end of every row until the sides of the square match the template (left). Cut the yarn of the first color 4 inches (10 cm) from the needles and join in the second color. Count the number of stitches on the needle.

IF A MULTIPLE OF 3 STS
Eyelet row: K3 sts * yo, K2tog, K1 *, rep from * to * until the end of the row.
IF A MULTIPLE OF 3 STS PLUS 2 STS
Eyelet row: K2 sts, * yo, K2tog, K1 *, rep from * to * until the end of the row.

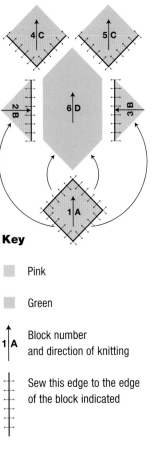

Key

Pink

Green

Block number and direction of knitting

Sew this edge to the edge of the block indicated

IF A MULTIPLE OF 3 STS PLUS 1 ST
Eyelet row: K2 sts, * yo, K2tog, K1 *, rep from * to * until the last 2 sts, K2tog.

Continue to work in the second color and knit two stitches together at the end of each row until no stitches remain.

Block D is an elongated basic hexagon; see page 42.

Make a slip knot and increase at the end of every row until the lower edges of the hexagon match the template (see page 94).

Work rows without increases or decreases until the vertical edges match the width of block B.

Knit two stitches together at the end of every row until no stitches remain.

Knitting a bootie (make two)

The blocks should be knitted separately using the chart (page 95) as a guide to the number and shape of the pieces.

Finishing

With the wrong side facing, pin out the pieces onto a blocking board or towel using the template as a guide. Check the pressing instructions on the ball band and, with a cool iron and a pressing cloth, gently press the pieces.

Join the pieces together using whip stitch (see page 23) or crochet (see page 24), following the order shown on the chart. The flatter the seams, the more comfortable they will be for the baby.

Thread the ribbon through the eyelets.

Variations

The basic bootie shape can be embellished in a number of ways. It is important to ensure that anything attached to the bootie is secured firmly and cannot be pried off by inquisitive fingers or gums.

Variation 1: with buttons and ribbon

Twist one end of a 2-inch (5-cm) length of ribbon and sew it to the other to create a figure of eight. Attach to block A and cover the join with a button or in this case two buttons, one over the top of the other.

Variation 2: with attach-later bobbles

Secure three attach-later bobbles to block A of the bootie.

TO MAKE AN ATTACH-LATER BOBBLE:
Make a basic square with sides measuring ⅞ inch (2 cm).

Cut the yarn leaving a 4-inch (10-cm) tail and thread it through a yarn needle. Using small running stitches, sew around the edges of the square. Pull the yarn tight and draw the edges together.

TO MAKE THE TIE:
Using the main color cast on sufficient stitches for a 10-inch (25-cm) length. On the next row, bind the stitches off. Thread the tie through the eyelets.

Variation 3: with satin stitch

Using a dressmaker's marker transfer a design onto interfacing. Iron the interfacing to the reverse of the block A. Embroider block A of the bootie with stitches such as satin stitch, lazy daisy, and French knots. Thread ribbon through the eyelets.

Patchwork ball

The crazy patchwork style of this soft ball is a very useful way to hide less-than-perfect seams. Using random embroidery stitches within the blocks will add to the charm. This ball can also be worked in scraps left over from other projects.

Size
Height: 6 inches (15 cm)

Materials
- For each of the five colors:
  ½ oz. (25g) of sport-weight yarn.
- Use needles one size smaller than those suggested on the ball band to produce a firm gauge.

For the ball shown:
Rowanspun 4-ply ⅞ oz. (25 g) balls
  - lime green   1
  - red   1
  - orange   1
  - Work using the yarn double throughout.
- Rowan felted tweed 1¾ oz. (50 g) balls
  - slate blue   1
- Jaeger matchmaker merino DK
  1¾ oz. (50 g) balls
  - flamingo pink 1
- A selection of embroidery silks and cottons in complementary colors.
- Washable soft toy filler.
- 1 pair of US 3 (3.25 mm) needles.

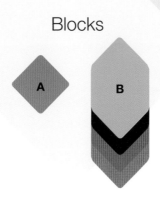

Templates
Use this template to check the size of blocks A and B.

For the suggested yarns, the number of stitches on the needle before decreasing should be:
14 stitches for blocks A and B.

Blocks

Blocks
The ball is made up of two different blocks.

Block A is a basic square; see page 20. Make a slip knot and increase at the end of every row until the sides of the square match the template (below, left).

Work one row with no increases.

Knit two stitches together at the end of every row until no stitches remain.

Block B is a basic hexagon; see page 42. Make a slip knot and increase at the end of every row until the lower edges of the hexagon match the template (left).

Work rows without increases or decreases until the vertical edges match the length of the lower edges of the hexagon.

Knit two stitches together at the end of every row until no stitches remain.

Center strip is a strip that joins the two halves of the ball.

Calculate the number of stitches required to make the strip half the width of the edge of block A, using the table on page 25. Cross reference the number of diagonal stitches on block A before decreasing begins, with the edge stitch count given, halve this number and, if necessary, round it up to the nearest whole number. Cast on this number of stitches using the cable method.

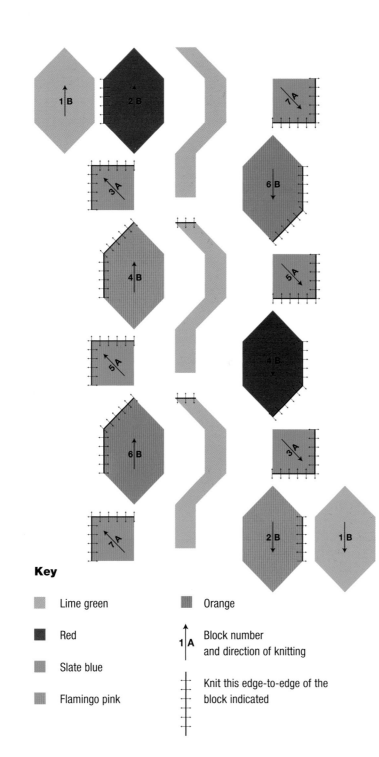

Key

Lime green

Red

Slate blue

Flamingo pink

Orange

1|A Block number
and direction of knitting

Knit this edge-to-edge of the
block indicated

* **STRAIGHT SECTION**

Work rows without increases or decreases until the vertical edges match the length of one of the edges of block A.

RIGHT SLOPING SECTION

Row 1: Inc, k to the end of the row.

Row 2: Knit.

Row 3: Inc, k to the end of the row.

Row 4: K2togtbl, k to the end of the row.

Repeat the last two rows until the edges match the length of one of the edges of block A.

Repeat the straight section.

LEFT SLOPING SECTION

Row 1: Knit

Row 2: Inc, k to the end of the row.

Repeat the last two rows.

Row 3: Knit

Row 4: K2togtbl, k to the end of the row.

Row 5: K2togtbl, k to the end of the row.

Row 6: Inc, k to the end of the row.

Repeat the last two rows until the edges match the length of one of the edges of block A.

Next row: K2togtbl, k to the end of the row.

Next row: Knit

Repeat the last two rows.*

Repeat from * to * twice more.

Attach-later bobble is a basic square with the edges drawn together; see page 96. Knit two in each of the block B colors.

Firmly secure the bobbles to the center of each block B.

Knitting the ball

The ball is worked in two halves with a center strip. The blocks can be knitted separately and joined by whip stitch, (see page 23), or crochet (see page 24), following the order shown on the chart (see page 98).

To knit the shapes together, see Joining shapes as you work, page 25. Start with block 1 and join the shapes to those to the left by picking up a stitch from the edge of the other square. Blocks 2–7 all join to the last block knitted and block 1.

Finishing

With the wrong side facing, pin out the pieces in sections to a blocking board or towel using the templates as a guide. Then check the pressing instructions on the ball bands and, starting with a cool iron and a pressing cloth, gently press the pieces.

Leaving one seam, join the pieces together using mattress stitch; see page 23. Stuff the ball with washable filler and close the last seam.

Embellish the seams and surface of the ball using complementary colors, and feather, lazy daisy, and chain stitch.

Blue and white

The basic square and the two-color basic square lend themselves to many traditional quilting patch designs. These patches can either be used singly or grouped to create a variety of designs.

Size
Cushion one: 12 inches (30 cm) × 12 inches (30 cm)
Cushion two: 16 inches (40 cm) × 16 inches (40 cm)
Afghan: 40 inches (1 m) × 54 inches (1.37 m)

Materials
- Cushion one, for each color: 3½ oz. (100 g) balls of a double knitting weight yarn.
- Cushion two, for each color: 5 oz. (140 g) balls of a double knitting weight yarn.
- Afghan for each colors: 15 oz. (420 g) balls of a double knitting weight yarn.
- To create a firm gauge in the chosen yarn, use needles one or two sizes smaller than those suggested on the ball band.

For the two cushions and afghan shown:
Jaeger aqua cotton 1¾ oz. (50 g) balls
    white   19
    blue   19
- Four ½-inch (12-mm) buttons.
- 1 pair of US 6 (4 mm) needles.

Blocks
These cushions and afghan are made up of five different blocks, but only three different constructions.

Blocks A and B are the same construction, but block B is larger.

Blocks C and D are the same construction, but block D is larger.

Templates
Use the smaller template to check the size of blocks A and C, and the larger template to check the size f blocks B, D, and E.

For the suggested yarns, the number of stitches on the needle before decreasing should be:
23 stitches for block A,
44 stitches for block B,
16 stitches for center square of block C,
32 stitches for center square of block D.

The number of stitches to be picked up along the edge should be:
11 stitches for blocks C,
23 stitches for blocks D and E.

Blocks

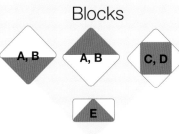

Blocks A and B are two-color basic squares; see page 20. Make a slip knot and increase at the end of each row until the sides of the square match the template (below, left). Cut the yarn of the first color and join the second color.

Work one row with no increases. Continue to work in the second color and knit two stitches together at the end of every row until none remain.

Blocks C and D are smaller squares with stitches picked up along each edge and knitted to create a square the same size as blocks A or B.

Starting with the center square, calculate the number of diagonal stitches, using the table on page 25. Find the number of diagonal stitches on block A or B before decreasing begins the edge stitch count is the total number of diagonal stitches.

Make a slip knot and increase at the end of every row until the calculated diagonal stitch count is reached.

*Work one row with no increases. Knit two stitches together at the end of every row until no stitches remain.

Calculate the number of stitches along each edge using the table on page 25 and pick up the stitches in the second color, see page 25.

Knit two stitches together at the end of every row until no stitches remain.

Repeat for each edge.

Block E is half of block C or D. Work as for block C or D from *, but casting on the number of diagonal stitches.

Knitting cushion one

FRONT

The blocks can be knitted separately and whip stitched (see page 23) or crocheted (see page 24) together later, following the order shown on the chart (below).

To knit the shapes together, see Joining shapes as you work, page 25. Start with block 1 and join the shapes to those to the left by picking up a stitch from the edge of the other square.

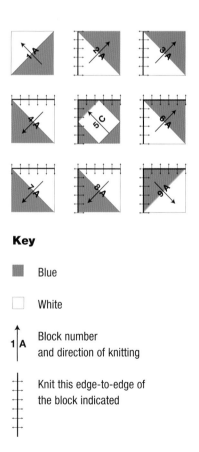

Key

■ Blue

□ White

1|A Block number and direction of knitting

┼┼┼ Knit this edge-to-edge of the block indicated

BACK

The back is made up of two rectangles joined together to make a square the same size as the front.

To knit a rectangle, see page 30.

FIRST RECTANGLE

** Make a slip knot in blue and increase at the end of every row for 8 rows.

Join in the second color and work the following stripe sequence.

*2 rows white
4 rows blue
2 rows white
2 rows blue
2 rows white
4 rows blue
2 rows white
8 rows blue *

From * to * forms the pattern; repeat throughout.

Continue increasing at the end of each row until the edge measures 6 inches (15 cm).**

Next row: K to the last st, inc.
Next row: K to the last 2 sts, K2tog. Repeat the last two rows until the side of the rectangle measures 12 inches (30 cm).

Knit two stitches together at the end of every row until no stitches remain.

SECOND RECTANGLE

Work as for first rectangle from ** to **.
Next row: K to the last 2 sts, K2tog.
Next row: K to the last st, inc.

Continue, following the stripe sequence and repeat the last two rows until the side of the rectangle measures 12 inches (30 cm)

Knit two stitches together at the end of every row until no stitches remain.

BACK FLAP

The back flap is a single right-angle triangle knitted to the width of the cushion with a single buttonhole 1 inch (2.5 cm) from the slip knot.

Make a slip knot in blue and increase at the end of every row for 1 inch (2.5 cm), ending with an odd number of stitches on the needle.

Buttonhole row: Knit to the center 3 sts, bind off 3 sts, and continue to the end of the row, increasing into the last stitch.

Next row: Knit to the bound-off stitches, cast on 3 sts to complete the buttonhole, and continue to the last stitch, increase.

Continue increasing at the end of each row until the width of the work is 12 inches (30 cm), and bind off.

Finishing

With the wrong side facing, pin out the pieces onto a blocking board or towel using the template as a guide. Check the pressing instructions on the ball band and, with a cool iron and a pressing cloth, gently press the pieces.

Join the front blocks if they have not been knitted together and weave all the ends into the seams.

Join the back pieces together using mattress stitch (see page 23) taking care to match the stripes.

Join the front side and bottom edges to the back by using mattress stitch.

Join the back flap to the front using whip stitch (see page 23).

Attach a button to the back to align with the buttonhole on the back flap.

Knitting cushion two

FRONT

Follow instructions for cushion one, using the chart below.

Block E is used in pairs and each can either be knitted separately or the upper block can be knitted by picking up the number of stitches to be cast on along the top edge of the lower block.

It takes practice to pick up stitches and knit on from a shape and to get sharp corners. Block E can also be divided in two vertically to make two blocks of A.

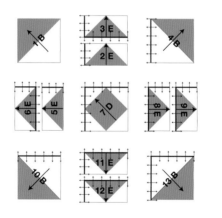

Key

Blue

White

1|A Block number
and direction of knitting

Knit this edge-to-edge of
the block indicated

BACK

The back is made up of a slip stitch pattern knitted with shaping as for the basic square.

Make a slip knot in white and increase at the end of every row until there are 7 sts on the needle.

Pattern row 1: *K1, sl1 purlwise* repeat from * to * to the last st, inc.

Pattern row 2: K2 *yf sl1 purlwise, yb, K1* repeat from * to * to the last 2 sts, yf sl1 purlwise, yb, inc.

Pattern rows 3–4: Knit.

Repeat these 4 rows until the edge measures 16 inches (40 cm).

Keeping the pattern correct, knit two stitches together at the end of every row until no stitches remain.

BACK FLAP

The back flap is a single right-angle triangle knitted to the width of the cushion with three buttons up the center.

Make a slip knot in blue and increase at the end of every row for 1 inch (2.5 cm), ending with an odd number of stitches on the needle.

***Buttonhole row:** Knit to the center 3 sts, bind off 3 sts, and continue to the end of the row, increasing into the last stitch.

Next row: Knit to the bound-off stitches, cast on 3 sts to complete the buttonhole, and continue to the end, increasing into the last stitch.

Continue increasing at the end of each row until the distance from the last buttonhole is 2½ inches (6 cm), ending with an odd number of stitches on the needle.*

Repeat from * to *.

Repeat the buttonhole row and next row once more.

Continue increasing at the end of each row until the width of the work is 16 inches (40 cm), and bind off.

Finishing

Follow the instructions for cushion one but make only one back piece.

Variations

The blocks used for the Blue and White projects can be created using beads to create the contrast color.

Thread the yarn with beads.

Every other row before working each stitch, slide a bead along the yarn so it is tight against the right needle.

The pattern used for the back of cushion two slips a stitch purlwise over two rows. This can give the illusion of more than one color being used along a row. In the example below, the first stitches and the first two pattern rows were worked in red, then the next two rows were worked in white and finally the next two rows were worked in blue.

Knitting an afghan

Both cushions one and two can be
used to create a matching afghan. In
the diagram (right) cushion two front
sections have been edged with blocks
half the size of block B.

Joining shapes as you work (see
page 27) will make the wrong side
of the afghan less obvious. Start
with blocks at the top left and join the
shapes to those to the left by picking
up a stitch from the edge of the
other square.

For a more portable project, knit the
blocks separately.

Finishing

Block and press as for cushion one.

Join the blocks together and weave
all the ends into the seams.

EDGING

With the blue yarn and right side facing,
pick up and knit 11 rows along a long
edge, inc in the last st of each row.
Bind off.

Repeat along the opposite edge.

Repeat for top and bottom edges of
the afghan, but do not include the
edging on the long edges.

Sew the border edges together at
the corner, working from the inside out,
and easing them together.

Geometric scarf

Size
30 inches (84 cm) × 9½ inches (24 cm)

Materials
For each of the three colors:
- 1 × 1¾ oz. (50 g) balls of a worsted-weight yarn.
- To create a soft drape in the chosen yarn, use needles one or two sizes larger than those suggested on the ball band.

For the scarf shown:
- Rowan kid classic 1¾ oz. (50 g) balls
  - dark gray   1
  - pink   1
- Jaeger luxury tweed 1¾ oz. (50 g) balls
  - gray   1
- 1 pair of US 9 (5.5 mm) needles.

Blocks
This scarf is made up of three different square or half-square blocks.

A scarf is a good introduction to modular knitting. Think of all those lovely alpacas, mohairs, and cashmeres that feel so good against the skin! Buy as much luxury yarn as you can and supplement it with odd remnants.

Template
Use this template to check the size of blocks A, B, and C.

For the suggested yarns, the number of stitches on the needle before decreasing should be 11 stitches for blocks A and C, and 22 sts for block B

Blocks

Block A is a right-angle triangle; see page 32. Make a slip knot and increase at the end of every other row, starting with the second row, until the sides of the triangle match the template (below, left). End a row with an increase. Work one row with no increase.

Knit two stitches together at the end of every other row until no stitches remain.

Block B is a two-color basic square with a slip-stitch pattern on the decrease rows. Make a slip knot in the first color and increase at the end of every row until the sides of the square match the template (left). Cut the first color and join in the second color.

Work one row with no increases.

Continue to work in the second color.

Row 1 (RS): Knit to the last 2 sts, K2tog.
Row 2: * K1, yf, sl1 knitwise, yb * Rep from * to * to the last 2 sts, K2tog.
Row 3: Knit to the last 2 sts, K2tog.
Row 4: * K2, yf, sl1 knitwise, yb * rep from * to * to the last 2 sts, K2tog.

Repeat rows 1–4 until no stitches remain.

Block C is a one-color vertical half-square similar to block A. Make a slip knot and increase at the end of every other row, starting with the first row, until the sides of the triangle match the template (left). End with a row with an increase.

Work one row with no increase.

Knit two stitches together at the end of every other row until none remain.

Knitting the scarf

The blocks can be knitted separately and whip stitched (see page 23) or crocheted (see page 24) together later, following the order shown on the chart (right).

To knit the shapes together and produce a neater reverse side, see Joining shapes as you work, page 25. Start with block 1 and join the shapes to those to the left by picking up a stitch from the edge of the other square.

Finishing

With the wrong side facing, pin out the pieces to a blocking board or towel using a copy of the templates as a guide. Then check the pressing instructions on the ball bands and, starting with a cool iron and a pressing cloth, gently press the pieces.

Join the blocks if they have not been knitted together and weave all the ends into the seams.

Make and cut the pom-pom (see page 86). Cut a piece of card the same length as the tassel plus a ½ inch (1.2 cm). Wrap the tassel yarn around the card until the skirt is the desired thickness. Secure the tassel near the top edge with a length of yarn. Tie this then round the center of the pom-pom. Trim the tassel skirt. Repeat five times.

Attach the tassels to the on-point squares on the ends of the scarf.

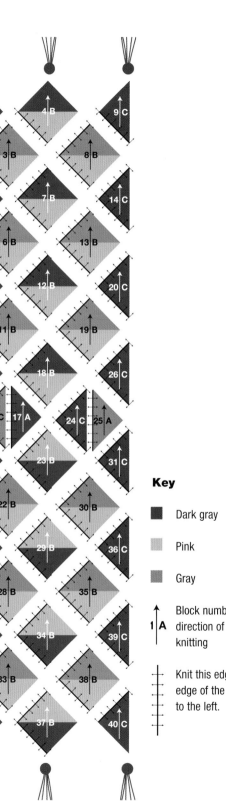

Key

- Dark gray
- Pink
- Gray

1 A Block number and direction of knitting

Knit this edge-to-edge of the block to the left.

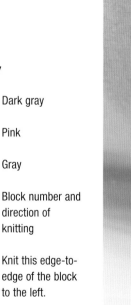

Baby hats

Size
Head circumference
Baby: 16 inches (40.5 cm)

Materials
- For each of the colors:
  1½ oz. (42 g) of a sport-weight yarn.
- To create a medium drape in the chosen yarn, use needles suggested on the ball band and experiment until the correct gauge has been achieved.

For the baby hat shown:
- Rowan cashcotton 4-ply 1¾ oz. (50 g) balls
  - pink   1
  - green   1
- 1 pair of US 5 (3.75 mm) needles.
- US 2 (2.75 mm) circular needle.

Blocks
This hat is made up of two different shapes: a kite, and a half-square block.

Block A is a kite shape which uses the different stitch proportion of stockinette stitch to create a different triangle shape. The kite shape is knitted partially in stockinette stitch and partially in garter stitch.
Cast on 3 sts.
Row 1: Knit.
Row 2: Purl.
Row 3: K1, M1, K1, M1, K1.
Work 3 rows in stockinette stitch.
Row 7: K2, M1, K1, M1, K2.
Repeat the last 4 rows, increasing

The crown is made up of radiating kite shapes in stockinette stitch. Create your own design by using any stitch with a short stitch and row repeat. Be careful if you use a pattern such as a twist as it may cause the crown to peak and sit high on the head. This can be avoided by knitting an extra round of basic square blocks.

Baby hat templates

Use these templates to check the size of blocks A and B.

For the suggested yarns, the number of stitches on the needle before decreasing should be 17 stitches for blocks A and B.

Blocks

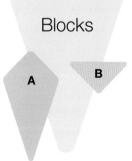

A   B

either side of the center stitch every fourth row, until the sides of the kite match the template (below, left).
End with a knit (RS) row.
Working in garter stitch, knit two stitches together at the end of every other row until no stitches remain.

Block B is a half-square or a right-angle triangle; see page 29.
Make a slip knot and increase at the end of every row until the sides of the square match the template.
Cut yarn, leaving a 4-inch (10-cm) tail.

Knitting the baby hat
Use the larger needles. The blocks can either be knitted separately or whip stitched (see page 23), following the order shown on the chart (on page 110). To knit the shapes together, see Joining shapes as you work, page 25. Start with block 1 and join the shapes to those to the left by picking up a stitch from the edge of the other square.
When each block B is completed, transfer the stitches onto the slightly smaller sized circular needle.

RIM
Count the number of stitches on the circular needle. If there is an odd number, knit two stitches together somewhere in the following row.
Using the green yarn, work ½ inch (12 mm) in stockinette stitch, working back and forth on the needle.

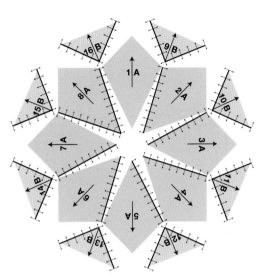

Key

Green

Pink

1 | A — Block number
and direction of knitting

Knit this edge-to-edge of
the block indicated

Cut the yarn, leaving a 4-inch
(10-cm) tail.

Join in the pink yarn, work 1 row in
pattern as set.

Rejoin the green yarn, work ½ inch
(12 mm) in pattern set.

Work in rib as follows.

Next row: * K1, P1 *, rep from * to * to
the end of the row.

Repeat the last row until the rib
pattern measures 1 inch (2.5 cm).

Bind off loosely.

Finishing

With the wrong side facing, pin out the
pieces onto a blocking board or towel,
using a copy of the template as a
guide. Check the pressing instructions
on the ball band and, starting with a
cool iron and a pressing cloth, gently
press the pieces.

Join the blocks if they have not been
knitted together and weave all the ends
into the seams.

Join the rim seam using mattress
stitch; see page 23.

Knitting the jester hat

This is a variation on the baby hat with
eight shapes in each round, and with a
point added to the crown. Work from
the center out as follows:

The first round is worked as for the
baby hat with a block similar to block
A, but with the increases every eighth
row. Once the correct width is achieved
the decreases are worked in either
green or orange yarn; alternating
around the crown.

The second round are basic squares
in red. Pick up stitches (see page 27),
along the diagonal of each basic
square using yellow yarn, knit one row

and decrease at the end of each row
until no stitches remain.

The third round is made up of half-
square blocks of alternating orange and
green. Do not bind off the stitches.

RIM

The stitches from the blocks in round
three were transferred onto a circular
needle. They were worked in red
stockinette stitch for ½ inch (12 mm)
and then rib as for the baby hat.

To create a second row of points on
round three, use the red yarn to pick
up stitches from one triangle point to
the next. Knit one row and decrease at
the end of each row until no stitches
remain.

Repeat three more times round the
crown; once for each pair of points.

Finishing

Follow instructions for the baby hat.

Adult hat

Size
Head circumference
Adult: 20 inches (50 cm)

Materials
- For each of the colors:
1½ oz. (42 g) of a sport-weight yarn.
- To create a medium drape in the chosen yarn, use needles suggested on the ball band and experiment until the correct gauge has been achieved.

For the adult hat shown:
- Rowan felted tweed 1¾ oz. (50 g) balls

  brown 1

  ruby 1

  mustard 1
- 1 pair of US 5 (3.75 mm) needles.
- US 2 (2.75 mm) circular needle.

Blocks
This hat is made up of three different shapes: a kite, a square block, and a half-square block.

Block A is a kite shape which uses the stitch proportion of stockinette stitch to create a different triangle shape. The kite shape is knitted partly in garter stitch and partly in stockinette stitch. Cast on 3 sts.
Row 1: Knit.
Row 2: Purl.
Row 3: K1, M1, K1, M1, K1.
Work 3 rows in stockinette stitch.

Hats are the perfect way to use up the odds and ends from your yarn stash. Only small amounts are required for this hat, which will allow you to mix and match different weights and textures to complement your favorite outfit.

Adult hat templates

Use this template to check the size of block A. Use the square template (above, left) to check the size of blocks B and C.

For the suggested yarns, the number of stitches on the needle before decreasing should be 26 stitches for blocks A, B, and C.

Blocks

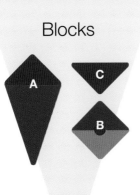

Row 7: K2, M1, K1, M1, K2.
Repeat the last 4 rows, increasing either side of the center stitch every fourth row, until the sides of the kite match the template (left).
Cut the yarn of the first color, leaving a 4-inch (10-cm) tail.
Join in the second color.
Knit 1 row.
Working in garter stitch, knit two stitches together at the end of every other row until no stitches remain.

Block B is two-color basic square (see page 28), with an attach-later bobble. Make a slip knot and increase at the end of every row until the sides of the square match the template (left), ending with a right side. Cut the yarn of the first color and join in the second color.
Work one row with no increases.
Continue to work in the second color and knit two stitches together at the end of every row until no stitches remain.

TO MAKE AN ATTACH-LATER BOBBLE:
Make a basic square with sides measuring ⅞ inch (2 cm).
Cut the yarn, leaving a 4-inch (10-cm) tail and thread it through a yarn needle. Using small running stitches, sew around the edges of the square. Pull the yarn tight and draw the edges together.
Attach to the center of the block.

Block C is a half-square or a right-angle triangle; see page 32.
Make a slip knot and increase at the end of every row until the sides of the square match the template (on page 111).

Cut yarn, leaving a tail of 4-inches (10-cm).

Knitting the adult hat

Use the larger needles. The blocks can be knitted separately and whip stitched (see page 23), following the order shown on the chart (right). To knit the shapes together, see Joining shapes as you work, page 25. Start with block 1 and join the shapes to those to the left by picking up a stitch from the edge of the other square.

When each block C is completed, transfer the stitches onto a slightly smaller sized circular needle.

RIM

Count the number of stitches on the circular needle. If there is an odd number, knit two stitches together somewhere in the following row.

Using the brown yarn, work ½ inch (12 mm) in stockinette stitch, working back and forth on the needles.

Cut the yarn, leaving a 4-inch (10-cm) tail.

Join in the ruby yarn, work 1 row in pattern as set.

Rejoin the brown yarn, work ½ inch (12 mm) in pattern as set.

Work in rib as follows.

Next row: * K1, P1 *, rep from * to * to the end of the row.

Key

■ Brown

■ Ruby

■ Mustard

1|A Block number and direction of knitting

Knit this edge-to-edge of the block indicated

Repeat the last row until the work measures 1 inch (2.5 cm) from the start of the rib.

Bind off loosely.

Finishing

With the wrong side facing, pin out the pieces onto a blocking board or towel, using a copy of the template as a guide. Then check the pressing instructions on the ball band and starting with a cool iron and a pressing cloth, gently press the pieces.

Join the blocks if they have not been knitted together and weave all the ends into the seams.

Join the rim seam using mattress stitch; see page 23.

Bag

Make this bag in many colors and forms. Add beads between the stitches for an evening style; use looped fur stitch for a more wintry look; or embellish with chain stitch and beads, and team with leather straps for a more ethnic look.

Size

13 inches (32.5 cm) × 9 inches (23 cm)

Materials

For each of the four colors:

■ 1 oz. (28 g) of a double knitting-weight yarn.

■ To create a very firm gauge in the chosen yarn, use needles two sizes smaller than those suggested on the ball band.

For the bag shown:

■ Jaeger Extra fine merino DK
  1¾ oz. (50 g) balls
  brown   1
  gray   1

■ Rowan kid classic 1¾ oz. (50 g) balls
  rose   1

■ Jaeger matchmaker merino DK
  1¾ oz. (50 g) balls
  beige   1

■ 8 × 1 inch (24 mm) buttons

■ US 3 (3.25 mm) circular needle.

■ 1 pair of US 3 (3.25 mm) double-pointed needles.

■ 1 pair of US 5 (3.75 mm) needles.

Abbreviations

ML= Insert the right-hand needle into the next stitch on the left-hand needle as if to knit and draw the loop through without dropping the stitch off the left-hand needle. Bring the yarn to the front between the two needles and wind it clockwise around your free thumb. Take the yarn to the back of the work

between the needles, knit the stitch again, and then slip it off the left-hand needle. Slip both stitches onto the left-hand needle, give the loop a sharp tug, and work the stitches together through the backs of their loops.

Blocks

The bag is made up of four different square, triangular, or parallelogram blocks.

Block A is a one-color parallelogram; see page 40. Make a slip knot and increase at the end of every other row, starting with the first row, until the sides of the parallelogram match the template (left). End with a row with an increase.

Work an even number of rows with no increases, until the vertical sides of the parallelogram match the template.

Knit two stitches together at the end of the next row and every other row until no stitches remain.

Block B is a two-color parallelogram with a slip-stitch pattern. Only one color is worked at a time; the other is woven in on the reverse side of the work. Make a slip knot, and increase at the end of every other row, starting with the first row, until the sides of the parallelogram match the template (left). End a row with an increase.

Cut the yarn of the first color and join in the second color.

Work an even number of rows with

Template

Use this template to check the size of blocks A, B, C, and D.

For the suggested yarns, the number of stitches on the needle before decreasing should be 12 stitches for blocks A and B, 21 sts for block C 23 sts for block D

Blocks

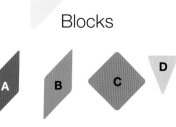

no increases, until the vertical sides of the parallelogram match the template.

Row 1 (RS): In the second color, yarn B, knit to the last 2 sts, K2tog.

Rejoin the first color, yarn A.

Row 2: Using yarn A, * K1, yf, sl1 knitwise, yb *, rep from * to * to the last 2 sts, K2tog, weaving yarn B along the row.

Row 3: Using yarn B, knit to the end of the row, weaving yarn A along the row.

Row 4: Using yarn A, * K2, yf, sl1 knitwise, yb *, rep from * to * to the last 2 sts, K2tog, weaving the yarn B along the row.

Repeat rows 1–4 until no stitches remain.

Block C is a basic square (see page 20), with every other row worked in looped fur stitch. Make a slip knot and increase at the end of every row for 6 rows.

Row 7: K1, * ML *, rep to the last stitch, inc.

Row 8: Knit to the last stitch, inc.

Repeat the last two rows until the sides of the square match the template (right).

Work one row as set by the repeat pattern but with no increases.

Continue to ML on every other row as set by the repeat pattern but knit two stitches together at the end of every row until no stitches remain.

The loops can be cut to create a fur texture or left in loops as shown here.

Block D is a 45-degree triangle; see page 32. Make a slip knot and increase at both ends of every fourth row, starting with the first row, until the sides of the parallelogram match the template (on page 114). End with a row with an increase.

Cut the yarn, leaving a 4-inch (10-cm) tail.

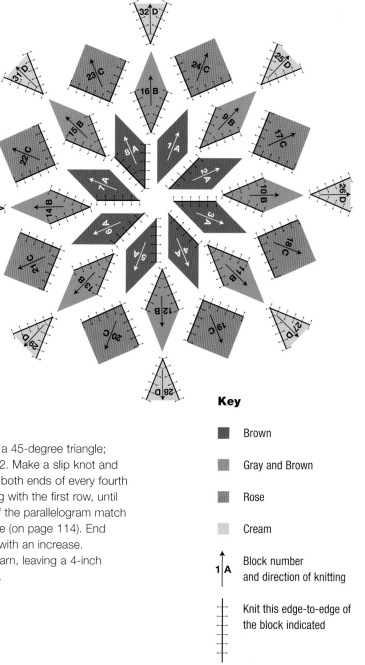

Key

- Brown
- Gray and Brown
- Rose
- Cream

1|A — Block number and direction of knitting

Knit this edge-to-edge of the block indicated

Knitting the bag

Use the larger needles. The blocks can be knitted separately and whip stitched (see page 23), or crocheted (see page 24) together later, following the order shown on the chart (left). For block B, the first color is gray and the second, brown.

To knit the shapes together, see Joining shapes as you work, page 25. Start with block 1 and join the shapes to those to the left by picking up a stitch from the edge of the other square.

When each block D is completed, transfer the stitches onto a slightly smaller circular needle.

TOP EDGE

Count the stitches on the circular needle and if there is an odd number, knit two stitches together somewhere in the following row as part of the rib. Using the rose yarn.

Next row: * K1, P1 *, rep from * to * to the end of the row.

Repeat the last row until the work measures 3 inches (7.5 cm) from the top of block D.

Bind off loosely.

I-CORD

Cast on 4 sts using brown yarn onto slightly smaller double-pointed needles.

Knit the stitches.

Slide the stitches along the needle until they are at the right-hand end and the yarn is on the left. Stretch the yarn across the back of the work and knit the first stitch of the previous row again, pulling the yarn tight across the back of the work. Continue knitting the remaining stitches on the row.

Repeat from * to * until the cord is 30 inches (75 cm) long.

STRAPS (MAKE TWO)

Cast on 9 sts using beige yarn onto slightly smaller double-pointed needles.

Row 1: Knit.

Row 2: Purl.

Repeat the last two rows until 10 rows have been completed.

Join in the rose yarn.

Work from * to * of the i-cord (left), knitting each row as follows:

Next row: * K1 rose, K1 beige * rep from * to * to the last st, K1 rose. Continue until the work measures 28 inches (70 cm).

Cut the rose yarn 4 inches (10 cm) from the needle.

Repeat the first 10 rows in beige.

Bind off.

Finishing

With the wrong side facing, pin out the pieces onto a blocking board or towel using a copy of the template as a guide. Then, check the pressing instructions on the ball band and, starting with a cool iron and a pressing cloth, gently press the pieces.

Join the blocks if they have not been knitted together and weave all the ends into the seams.

Fold the top edge over to the right side and stitch the top edge to the top edge of the round of block D shapes, leaving a small gap at the front.

Thread the i-cord through the gap and use to draw the bag closed.

Attach the first strap to the top inside edge of the bag 3 inches (7.5 cm) from either side of the front gap.

Flatten the bag slightly with the gap in the top edge to the center back and attach the second strap to align with the first on the back edge.

For extra security, a length of ¼-inch (6-mm) chain can be threaded and secured through the center of the i-cord straps.

Sew the buttons to the center of each block C.

Sweater

This garment is made up of mitered squares that are easy to join together as you knit. Because of the way it is made, this stockinette mitered square drapes better than the garter stitch basic square. Mitered squares tolerate more stitch combinations; so experiment.

Size
Imperial

CHEST SIZE	SQUARE EDGE	SQUARE DIAGONAL
34 inches	3⅛ inches	4⅜ inches
36 inches	3¼ inches	4½ inches
40 inches	3¾ inches	5⅛ inches
42 inches	4⅞ inches	5⅜ inches

Metric

CHEST SIZE	SQUARE EDGE	SQUARE DIAGONAL
86 cm	8 cm	11 cm
91 cm	8.5 cm	11.5 cm
102 cm	9.5 cm	13 cm
107 cm	10 cm	13.5 cm

Materials
- 1¾ oz. (50 g) balls of a sport-weight yarn.
  Main color   9 (10, 11, 11)
- To create a soft drape, use needles one size larger than those suggested on the ball band.

For the sweater shown:
- Rowan cashcotton DK 1¾ oz. (50 g) balls
  green   9 (10, 11, 11)
- Size 8 beads 2 oz. (50 g) pack
  cream   1
- 1 pair of US 7 (4.5 mm) needles
- 1 US 3 (3.25 mm) circular needle

Template
Choose the appropriate size square and use the template to check the size of blocks A, B, and C.

For the suggested yarns the number of stitches required for two edges of the square are:
34 inches (86 cm) 33 sts
36 inches (91 cm) 35 sts
40 inches (102 cm) 39 sts
42 inches (107 cm) 41 sts

Blocks

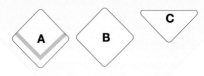

Abbreviations
Sl2tog, K1, Psso = slip two stitches together knitwise, knit 1, pass the slipped stitches over.
PB = place bead. Slide a bead along the yarn so it lies tight against the last stitch knitted, knit the next stitch.
K2togtbl = knit two stitches together through the back of the loops.

Blocks
This sweater is made up of one mitered block with three variations.

Block A is a one-color mitered square with beads. Thread the ball of yarn with beads. Use the ball band and the experience of your knitting gauge to calculate and work a test square to the correct size. Remember these stitches form two edges of the block.

Cast on, or cast on and pick up an odd number of stitches with an even number for each edge and the odd stitch in the center.
Row 1 (WS): Knit.
Row 2 (RS): K to the center 3 sts, sl2tog, K1, psso, k to the end of the row.
Row 3: Purl.
Repeat rows 2–3 until the two edges equal a quarter of the template edge, ending with a RS row and there are an even number of stitches on the needle.
Next row: * K1, PB *, rep from * to * to the last st, K1.

BACK

FRONT

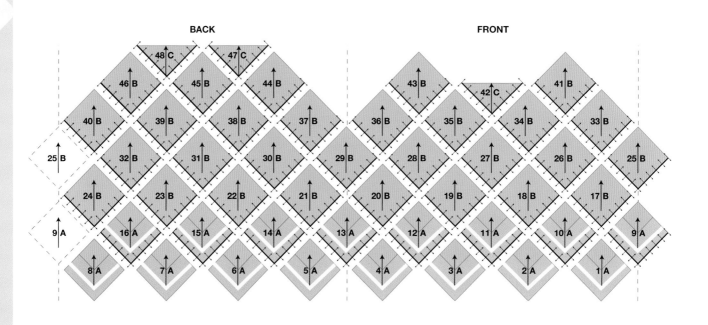

Key

green

Place bead

 1|A Block number and
direction of knitting

Knit this edge to the
edge of the block
indicated

SLEEVE

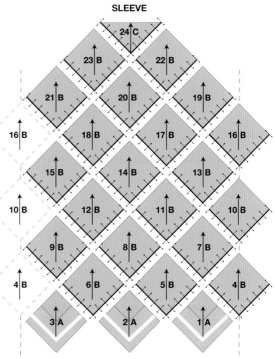

Next row (RS): K1, *yo, K2togtbl*, rep from * to * to the center 3 sts, sl2tog, K1, psso, *K2tog, yo*, rep from * to * to the last st, K1.

Next row: Purl.

Repeat the last 2 rows until the two edges equal half the template edge, ending with a WS row.

Next row: K to the center 3 sts, sl2tog, K1, psso, k to the end of the row.

Next row: Purl.

Repeat the last 2 rows until no stitches remain.

Block B is a one-color mitered square with no beads.

Cast on, or cast on and pick up an odd number of stitches with an even number for each edge and and the odd stitch in the center.

Row 1: Knit.

Row 2: K to the center 3 sts, sl2tog, K1, psso, k to the end of the row.

Row 3: Purl.

Repeat rows 2–3 until no sts rem.

Block C is a one-color mitered half square with no beads. Cast on or cast on and pick up an odd number of stitches with an even number for each edge and the odd stitch in the center picked up between the two blocks below.

Row 1: Knit.

Row 2 (RS): K1, K2togtbl, k to the center 3 sts, sl2tog, K1, psso, k to the last 3 sts, K2tog, K1.

Row 3: Purl.

Repeat rows 2–3 until no sts rem.

Knitting the sweater

The sweater front and back is worked in one cylindrical piece with block 1 on the first row of the front.

Row 1: Work block A 8 times.

Row 2: Start with block 9 and join the shapes to those below. For block 9 pick up half the number of stitches from the top edge of block 8, cast on the odd number stitch and pick up the remaining stitches from the edge of block 1.

Work block 9A.

Repeat for blocks 10–16.

For block 17, pick up half the number of stitches from the top edge of block 9, pick up the odd number stitch from the increase stitch loop of the point of block 1, and pick up the remaining stitches from the edge of block 10.

Work block 17B.

Repeat for blocks 18–48.

Continue to work the blocks as indicated, following the chart (left) until block 48 has been completed.

Sleeve (make 2)

The sleeve front and back is worked in one cylindrical piece.

Row 1: Work block A 3 times.

Row 2: Start with block 4 and join the shapes to those below. For block 4, pick up half the number of stitches from the top edge of block 3, cast on the odd number stitch and pick up the remaining stitches from the edge of block 1.

Work block 4B.

Repeat for block 5–6.

For block 7 pick up half the number of stitches from the top edge of block 4, pick up the odd number stitch from the increase stitch loop of the point of block 1 and pick up the remaining stitches from the edge of block 5.

Work block 7B.

Repeat for blocks 8–24.

Continue to work the sleeve following the chart (left) until block 24 has been completed, working the blocks as indicated.

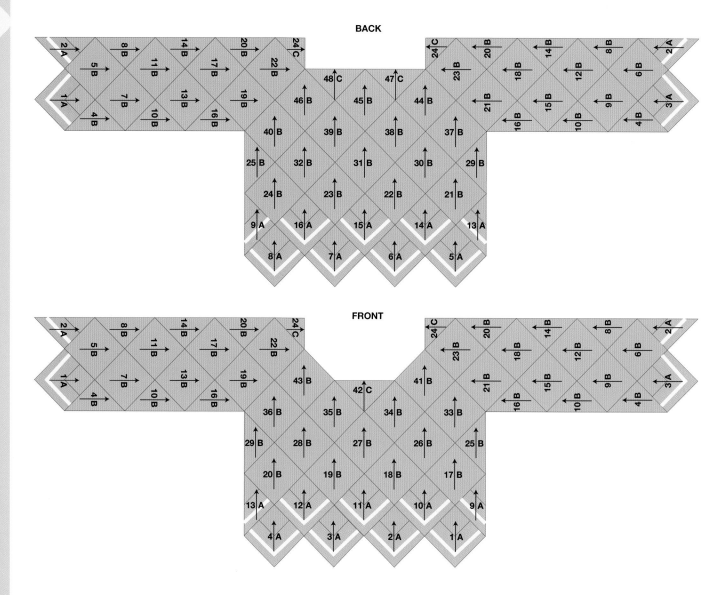

BACK

FRONT

Finishing

With the wrong side facing, lightly press all the pieces.

Join the sleeves to the sweater body using mattress stitch; see page 23, and the diagrams above as a guide.

Using the US 3 (3.25 mm) circular needle, pick up stitches around the neck, picking up an even number of stitches along the edges as before and using the table on page 25 to determine the number of stitches across the top of the B blocks.

Knit 4 rows in the round around the neckline. Loosely bind off.

Useful information

And, finally, some information that may be useful to have on hand as you explore the ideas in this book.

Yarns
The choice of yarns presented by manufacturers is enormous and enough to make any knitter want to get out her knitting needles. In general, using yarns from a manufacturer that has a reputation for quality will always make knitting a pleasure and the finished result better.

Knitted samples
Yarns used on pages 8–91.

Jaeger Siena 4-Ply
Fingering-weight yarn
100% mercerized cotton
Approx. 153 yds (140 m) per
1³/₄ oz. (50 g) ball

Rowan 4-Ply Cotton
Fingering-weight yarn
100% cotton
Approx. 186 yds (170 m) per
1³/₄ oz. (50 g) ball

Jaeger Matchmaker Merino 4-ply
Fingering-weight yarn
100% merino wool
Approx. 200 yds (183 m) per
1³/₄ oz. (50 g) ball

Rowan Cotton Glacé
Sport-weight yarn
100% cotton
Approx. 125 yds (115 m) per
1³/₄ oz. (50 g) ball

Jaeger Matchmaker Merino DK
Double knitting-weight yarn
100% merino wool
Approx. 131 yds (120 m) per
1³/₄ oz. (50 g) ball

Rowan Wool Cotton
Double knitting-weight yarn
50% merino wool, 50% cotton
Approx. 123 yds (113 m) per
1³/₄ oz. (50 g) ball

Project yarns
Yarns used on pages 94–121.

Jaeger Extra Fine Merino DK
Sport-weight yarn
100% extra fine merino wool
Approx. 137 yds (125 m) per
1³/₄ oz. (50 g) ball

Rowan Felted Tweed DK
Double-knitting-weight yarn
50% merino wool, 25% alpaca, 25% viscose/rayon
Approx. 191 yds (175 m) per
1³/₄ oz. (50 g) ball

Jaeger Luxury Tweed
Double knitting-weight yarn
65% merino lambswool, 35% alpaca
Approx. 197 yds (180 m) per
1³/₄ oz. (50 g) ball

Rowan Kid Classic
Worsted-weight yarn
70% lambswool, 26% kid mohair, 4% nylon
Approx. 153 yds (140 m) per
1³/₄ oz. (50 g) ball

Rowan Classic Yarns Cashcotton 4-Ply
Fingering-weight yarn
35% cotton, 25% polyamide, 18% angora, 13% viscose, 9% cashmere
Approx. 197 yds (180 m) per
1³/₄ oz. (50g) ball

Rowanspun 4ply
Fingering-weight yarn
100% pure new wool
Approx. 162 yds (148 m) per
⁷/₈ oz. (25 g) hank

Rowan Classic Yarns Cash cotton DK
Sport-weight yarn
35% cotton, 25% polyamide, 18% angora, 13% viscose,
9% cashmere
Approx. 130 yds (142 m) per
1³/₄ oz. (50 g) ball

Jaeger Matchmaker Merino DK
Double knitting-weight yarn
100% merino wool
Approx. 131 yds (120 m) per
1³/₄ oz. (50 g) ball

Jaeger Aqua Cotton
Double knitting-weight yarn
100% mercerized cotton
Approx. 116 yds (106 m) per
1³/₄ oz. (50 g) ball

Substituting yarns
The techniques and projects described in this book are particularly suited to the substitution of yarn.

There are several points to consider in order to successfully substitute yarns. First is its potential for wear and tear and the properties of different yarn compositions. Retailers are a rich source of information about their stock and often have sample swatches or finished projects in the store that can be examined. If the substituted yarn is of a similar weight and composition, then the question more often is how much yarn would be

required. The simplest way to calculate this is to work out the total yardage of the yarn specified (number of balls multiplied by yardage of one ball) and divide this by the yardage of one ball of the substituted yarn. Yardage information is given on most ball bands.

However, for all yarn substitutions, it is always a good idea to weigh a ball of yarn and, using the needles suggested on the ball band, knit a sample block. If this block does not feel or look right, adjust the needle size until the desired drape is achieved. Then either weigh the block or, if only one block is knitted, the ball to discover the percentage yardage of yarn used for one block.

Alternatively, unravel the knitted block and measure the length of the yarn used. Multiply this figure by the number of blocks, facings and notions to estimate the amount of yarn required in the pattern. The sooner this is done, the more likely it is to be possible to purchase more of the same yarn or a complementary yarn that may have been produced by the same manufacturer for that season.

Yarn definitions

There are no rules about the use of yarns. Weight terms are simply a way of describing the nature of a yarn to someone who hasn't seen it. Their uses can be mixed and matched, and the recommended needle sizes and gauge information ignored to achieve the desired effect.

Fingering-weight yarn

This is the lightest weight and often used for gossamer shawls or baby clothes. The recommended needle sizes range from US 0–3 and have a gauge of more than 27 stitches over 4 inches (10 cm).

Sport-weight yarn

This yarn is often used for lighter garments and may have the appearance of double knitting yarn, but because of its composition benefits from either being knitted on very small needles or with a slightly tighter tension. Sport-weight yarns are very good for dense stitch patterns because they don't become unyielding. The recommended needle sizes often range from US 4–6 and have a gauge of 22–26 stitches over 4 inches (10 cm).

Double knitting-weight yarn (DK weight)

This yarn is slightly heavier and denser than sport-weight yarn and produces a denser fabric than sport-weight yarn on simple stitch patterns. The recommended needle sizes often range from US 4–6 and have a gauge of 21–22 stitches over 4 inches (10 cm).

Worsted-weight yarn

This yarn tends to have the appearance of a chunky yarn, but it is spun with a lot of loft. It feels light and soft, and will produce garments that feel quite light but with more warmth than lighter yarn weights. It is excellent for afghans because it knit up quite quickly but doesn't have weight. The recommended needle sizes range from US 7–9 and have a gauge of 16–20 stitches over 4 inches (10 cm).

Chunky-weight yarn

This yarn is quite heavy and dense, and is useful for heavier outdoor garments and afghans. The recommended needle sizes often range from US 9–10^1/$_2$ and have a gauge of 14–15 stitches over 4 inches (10 cm).

Bulky-weight yarn

The bulk of this yarns means that it is often only suitable for simple stitch patterns, and its bulk does not necessarily translate into warmth. It is very quick to knit, with very few stitches for an average garment but the needle sizes mean that they can be unwieldy. The recommended needle sizes often range from US 10 and larger, with a gauge of less than 13 stitches over 4 inches (10 cm).

Abbreviations

Many of these entries appear in this book, though we have included others for reference when experimenting with stitch patterns for your shapes.

alt alternate
beg beginning/begin
cont continue
cm centimeter
Cr2 cross the number stated
C4B cable back the number stated
C4F cable forward the number stated
dec decrease
dp double pointed
foll/folls following/follows
g grams
in. inch
inc increase, knit into the front and back of the next stitch
k knit, see page 17
k2tog knit two stitches together
k2tog tbl knit two stitches together through the backs of the loops
MB make bobble
ML make loop; insert the right-hand needle into the next stitch on the left-hand needle as if to knit, draw the loop through without dropping the stitch off the left-hand needle. Bring the yarn to the front between the two needles and wind it clockwise around your free thumb. Take the yarn to the back of the work between the needles, knit the

stitch again and then slip it off the left-hand needle. Slip both stitches onto the left-hand needle, give the loop a sharp tug, and then work the stitches firmly together through the backs of their loops.
M1 make one; pick up the loop that lies between the stitch just knitted and the next by inserting the right needle from front to back. Transfer onto the left needle and work the stitch by inserting the needle into the back of the stitch.
oz. ounces
p purl, see page 18
patt pattern
PB place bead, using the method stated in the pattern
psso pass slipped stitch over
p2tog purl two stitches together
p2tog tbl purl two stitches together through the backs of the loops
rem remaining
rep/reps repeat/repeats
RS right side of work
sl knitwise slip knitwise; insert the right needle into the st/sts as if to knit but pass onto the right needle without winding the yarn around the needle
sl purlwise slip purlwise; insert the right needle into the st/sts as if to purl but pass onto the right needle without winding the yarn around the needle
ssk slip, slip, knit 2 stitches together
st/sts stitch/stitches

ST st stockinette stitch
sl2tog k1 psso slip two stitches together knitwise, knit 1, pass the slipped stitches over
tbl through the back of the loop/s
T2B twist 2 back
T2F twist 2 forward
WS wrong side of work
yb yarn back between the needles
yf yarn forward between the needles
yfon yarn forward and over needle to make a stitch
yo yarnover

★ repeat instructions between ★ as many times as instructed
[ ] repeat instructions between [ ] as many times as instructed

US and English terms

US	English
Bind off	Cast off
Gauge	Tension
Seed stitch	Moss stitch
Stockinette stitch	Stocking stitch

Conversions
Needle sizes

US size	Metric size	Canadian size
15	10	000
13	9	00
11	8	0
–	7.5 mm	1
10½	7	2
–	6.5 mm	3
10	6	4
9	5.5 mm	5
8	5	6
7	4.5 mm	7
6	4	8
5	3.75 mm	9
4	3.5 mm	–
3	3.25 mm	10
–	3	11
2	2.75 mm	12
1	2.25 mm	13
0	2	14

Index

Suppliers of Rowan Yarns and Jaeger Handknits

USA

Westminster Fibers Inc.
4 Townsend West
Suite 8
Nashua, NH 03063
Tel: 603 886 5041
Fax: 603 886 1056

Canada

Diamond Yarn
9697 St Laurent
Montreal
Quebec H3L 2N1
Tel: 514 388 6188

Diamond Yarn (Toronto)
155 Martin Ross
Unit 3
Toronto
Ontario M3J 2L9
Tel: 416 736 6111

Australia

Rowan at Sunspun
185 Canterbury Road
Melbourne
Victoria 3126
Tel: 03 9830 1609

UK

Rowan Yarns and Jaeger Handknits
Green Lane Mill
Holmfirth
West Yorkshire
HD9 2DX
Tel: 01484 681881
www.knitrowan.com

QUARTO WOULD LIKE TO THANK: Luise Roberts for designing projects on pages 94–122, and for her advice on other sections.

Heather Esswood for knitting the sweater, and for demonstrating techniques.

Jackie Jones for make up and hair.

Models: Tashi, at Models Direct, Sami Williamson, and Isabelle Crawford.

All photographs and illustrations are the copyright of Quarto Inc. While every effort has been made to credit contributors, Quarto would like to apologize should there have been any omissions or errors.